THE IMPRESSIONIST REVOLUTION

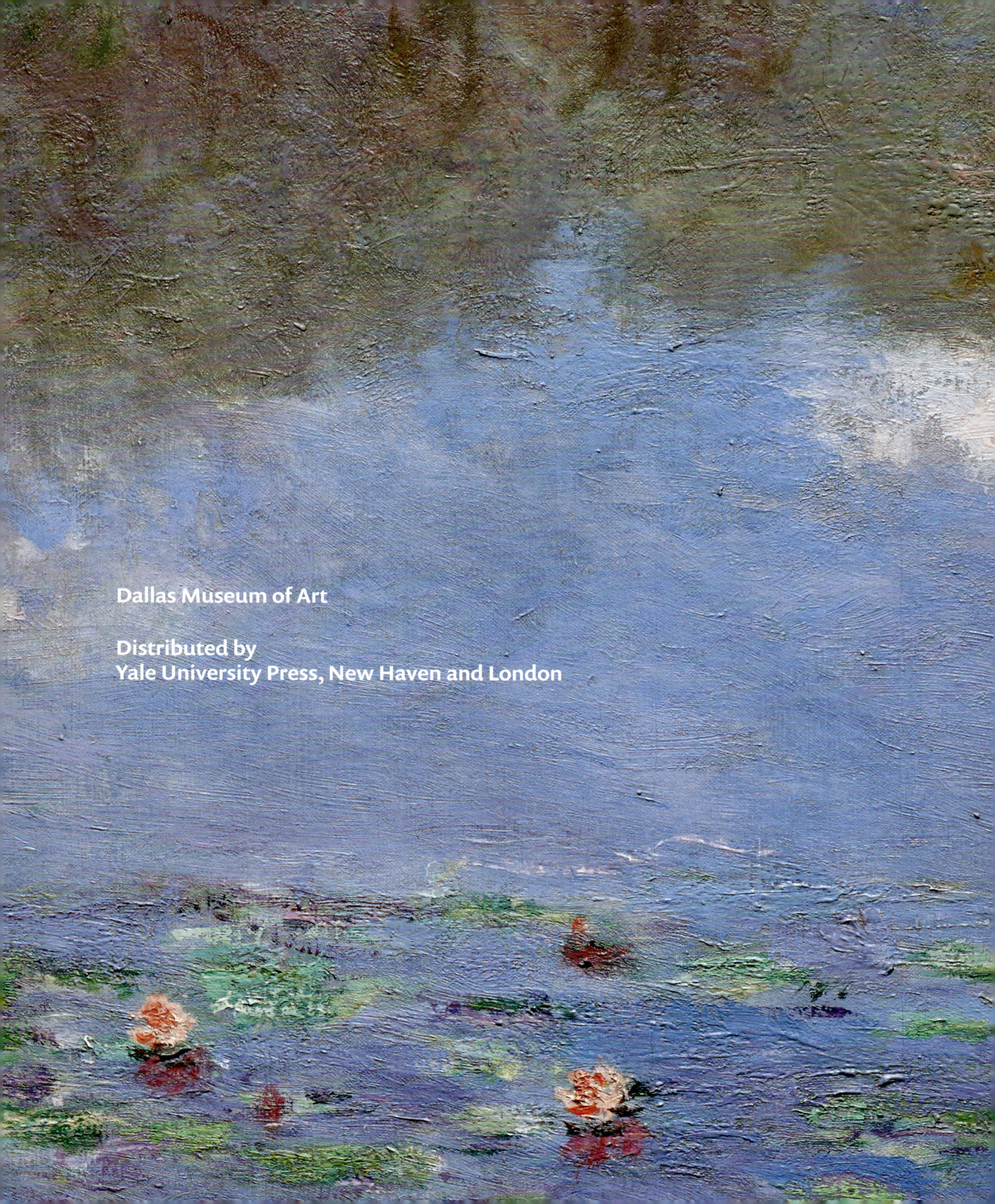
Dallas Museum of Art

Distributed by
Yale University Press, New Haven and London

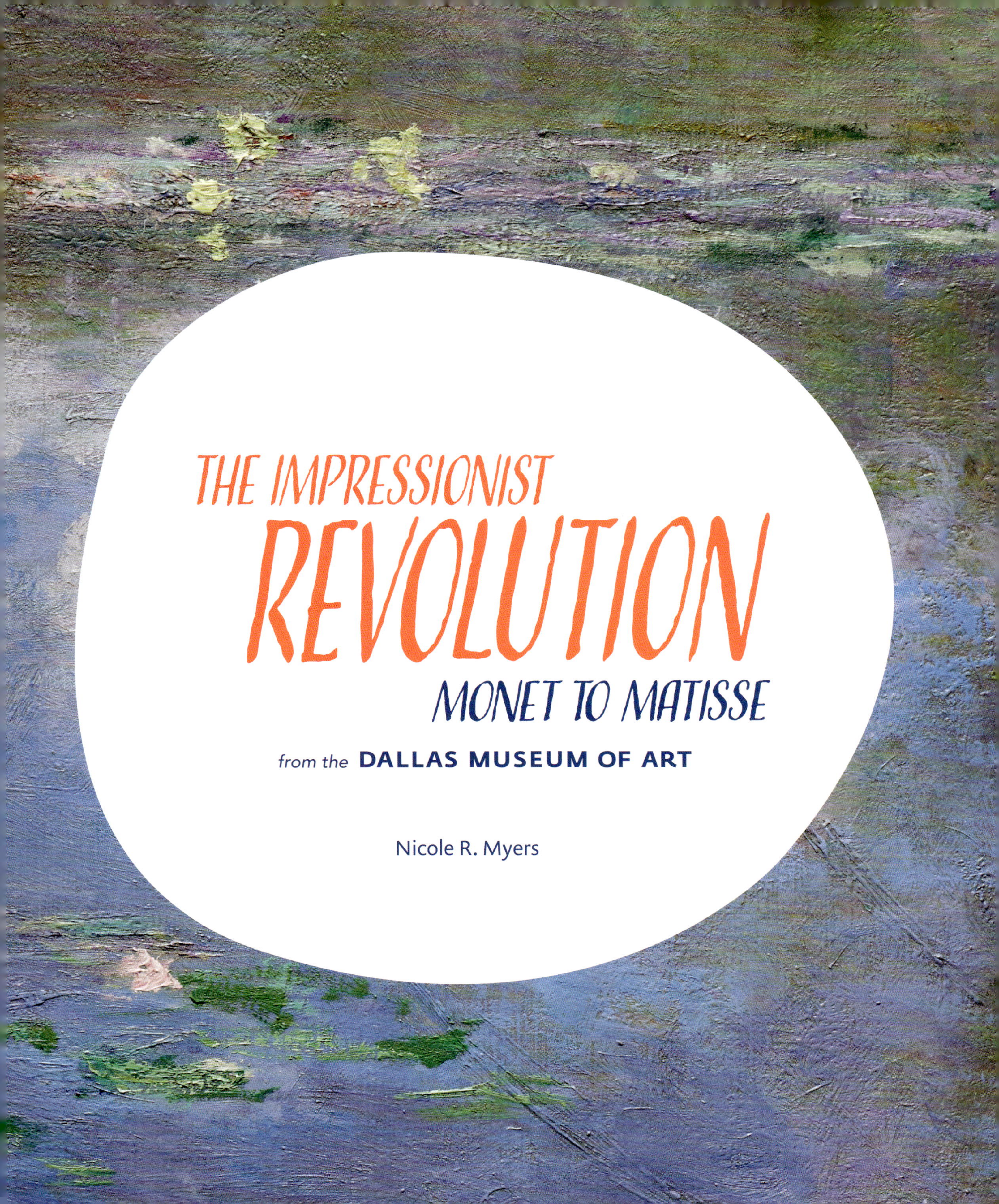

THE IMPRESSIONIST REVOLUTION

MONET TO MATISSE

from the DALLAS MUSEUM OF ART

Nicole R. Myers

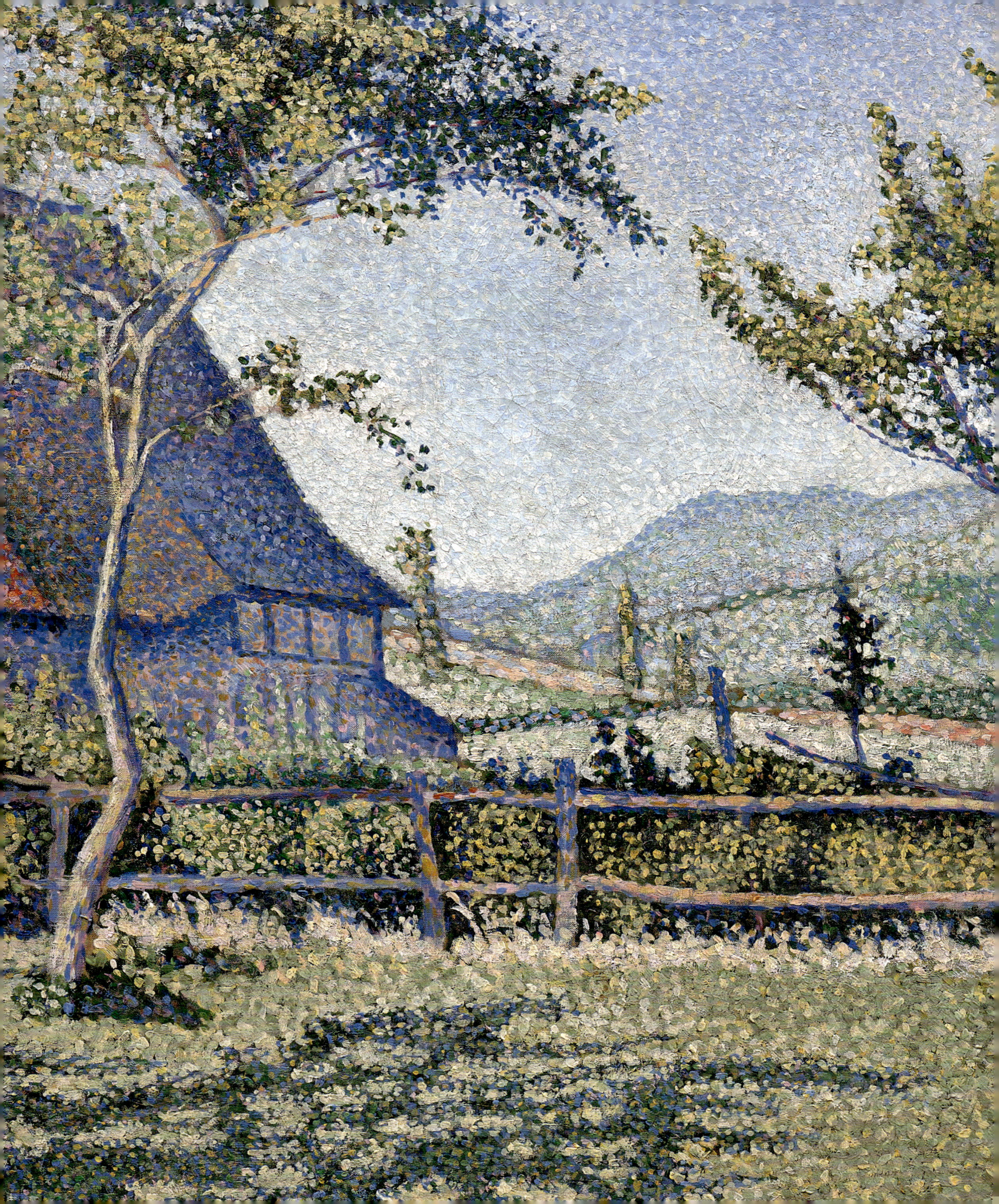

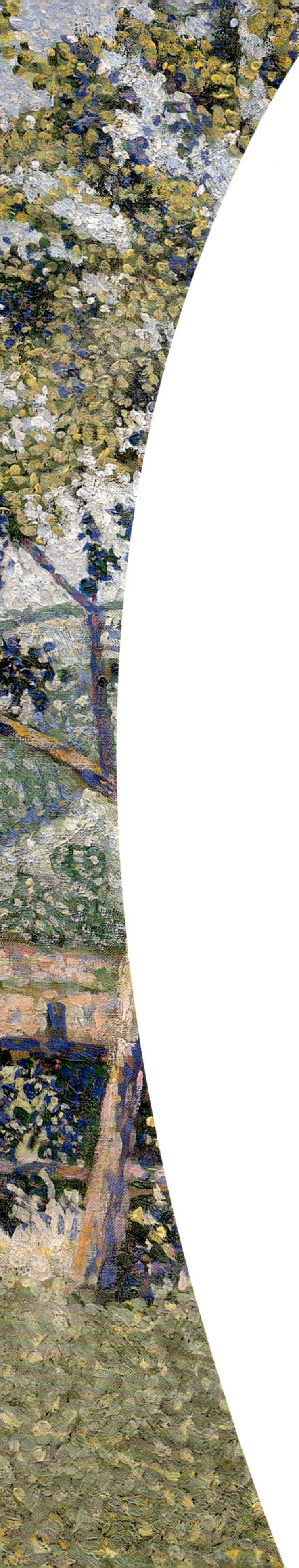

Contents

Director's Foreword

PRESENTED ENTIRELY THROUGH THE DALLAS MUSEUM OF ART'S EXCEPTIONAL HOLDINGS, *THE IMPRESSIONIST REVOLUTION: MONET TO MATISSE FROM THE DALLAS MUSEUM OF ART* RECOUNTS THE FASCINATING STORY OF IMPRESSIONISM FROM ITS BIRTH IN 1874 TO ITS LEGACY IN THE EARLY TWENTIETH CENTURY.

Following closely after the worldwide celebration of the 150th anniversary of the first Impressionist exhibition, *The Impressionist Revolution* is a testament to the movement's lasting significance, and to the Dallas community's enduring commitment to acquiring French avant-garde art. To tell the story of Impressionism and its long-lasting influence is to tell the story of some of this city's greatest acts of public philanthropy. The DMA's world-class collection of Impressionism, Post-Impressionism, and modernism is relatively young, the majority of the works having been acquired in the last three decades thanks to the brilliant foresight and generosity of the Munger Fund, Wendy and Emery Reves, the Foundation for the Arts, The Eugene and Margaret McDermott Art Fund, Inc., and Ralph and Cornelia Heins, among many others.

The Impressionist Revolution thus traces two parallel stories, both of which are recounted in this beautifully illustrated catalogue authored by Dr. Nicole R. Myers, Chief Curatorial and Research Officer and The Barbara Thomas Lemmon Senior Curator of European Art at the Dallas Museum of Art. Nicole played a major role not only in conceiving of and executing the exhibition and this accompanying volume, but also in expanding our holdings in this area with extraordinary acquisitions. Her dedication to researching, interpreting, and sharing her passion for this artwork is exceptional, and our museum is far better for it. I offer my sincerest congratulations to Nicole, as well as to Christine Burger, Emma Thompson, Meg Roppolo, and Shelby Bennett, her wonderful curatorial research team, whose contributions over the years can be seen on the exhibition walls and throughout this book. The exhibition has come to fruition thanks to the talents of the entire DMA staff, who assiduously work to bring each project to life for our visitors. Special thanks are due to the core exhibition team:

Sabrina Lovett, former Director of Collections, Exhibitions, and Interpretation; Amanda Dietz Brooks, Head of Exhibitions and Publications; Emily Schiller, Senior Manager of Interpretation; Emily Wiskera, Interpretation Specialist; Kate Aoki, former Head of

Exhibition Design; Ruth Bristow, former Exhibition Designer; Rachael Huszar, Exhibition Designer; Queta Moore Watson, Senior Editor; Peter Skow, Spanish Language Editor and Translator; Justin Penov, Head Preparator; Tricia Earl, Registrar for Loans; and Laura Eva Hartman, Paintings Conservator, who cleaned and restored many of the paintings expressly for this exhibition.

For their contributions to the creation of this publication, I extend my deep appreciation to Eric Zeidler, former Publications Manager, who expertly shepherded the initial phase of this project; Amanda Dietz Brooks, Head of Exhibitions and Publications; Veronica Treviño Salinas, Exhibitions and Publications Project Manager; Shelby Bennett, Curatorial Assistant for European, Islamic, and African Art; Meg Roppolo, former Curatorial Assistant for European, Islamic, and African Art; Christine Burger, former Research Assistant for European Art; and Emma Thompson, former Dedo and Barron Kidd McDermott Intern Fellow for European Art. I also wish to thank Queta Moore Watson for her meticulous editing of the catalogue; Mandy Engleman and Becca Winti of Boldface Studio for the book's attractive design and production; Friesens for the printing and binding; and Nicholas Geller and Carlin Cassel at Yale University Press, our distributor. Generous support for this exhibition comes from Texas Instruments and PNC Bank, as well as from the Freeman Family Exhibition Fund, Heritage Auctions, and Sewell Automotive, devoted partners whose enthusiasm helps the DMA bring art to our community in many ways, including sharing this story about Impressionism and its legacy with new audiences, both near and far.

On behalf of the Dallas Museum of Art, I dedicate this project to the Impressionist collective, whose innovations charted the course of modern art into the twentieth century and beyond, and to all who have worked tirelessly to build a superlative collection to be shared with art lovers around the world.

TAMARA WOOTTON FORSYTH
Interim Director/The Marcus-Rose Family Deputy Director

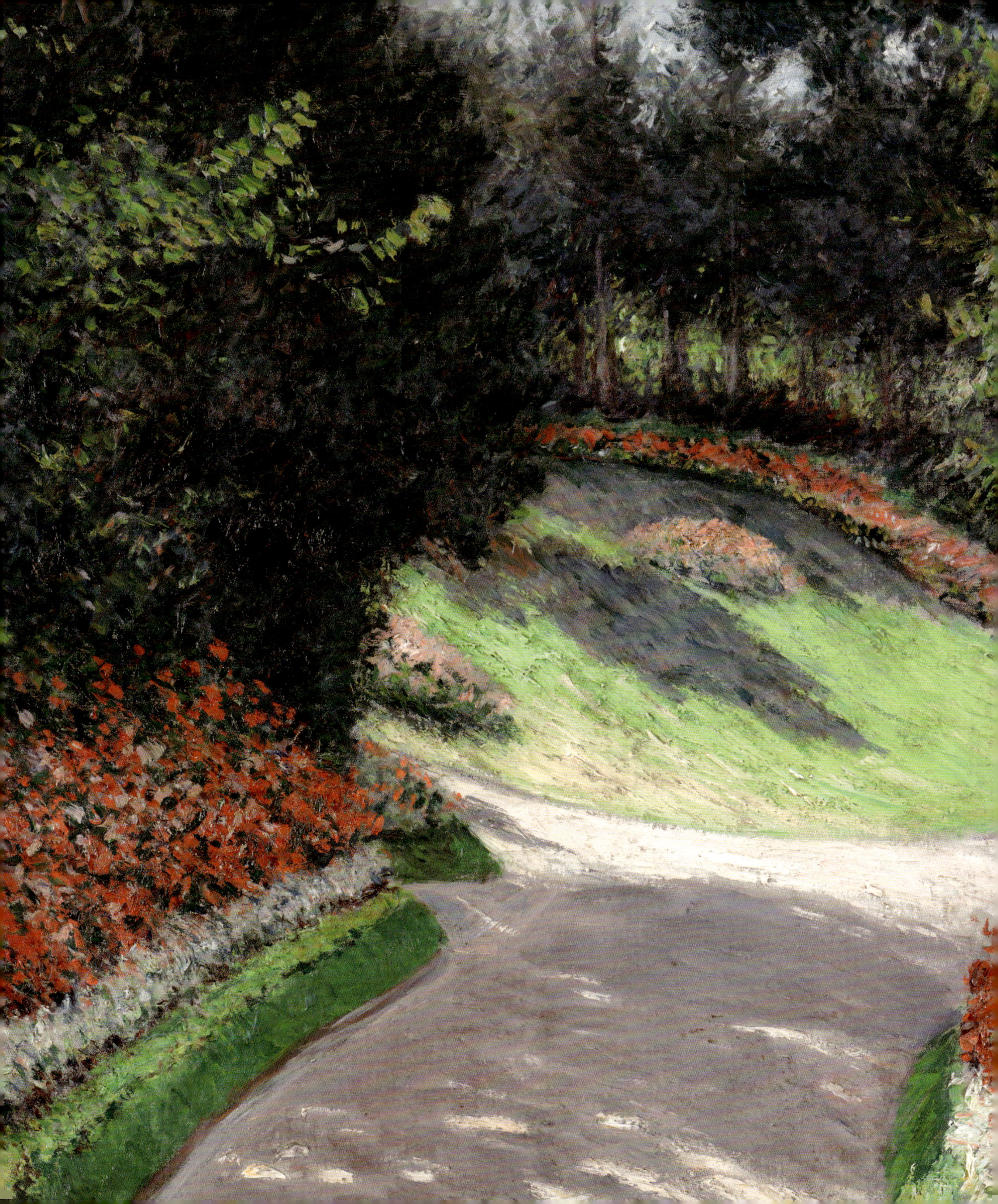

That 1870s Show

Nicole R. Myers

Impressionism is probably the most recognized kind of art around the world. It's hard to think of another type of art that is so popular, so beloved, so familiar that if I say the word *Impressionism*, many automatically envision water lilies by Claude Monet or ballet dancers by Edgar Degas. Impressionism is one of the truly rare instances where modern art made the leap from the high art world of museums to the so-called low art world of pop culture. This is particularly true in American culture, where Impressionist paintings have cameos in some of the most popular films of the twentieth century, including *Ferris Bueller's Day Off* (1986), *Titanic* (1997), and *The Thomas Crown Affair* (1999), and are reproduced on everything from soap wrappers and calendars to umbrellas and duvet covers.

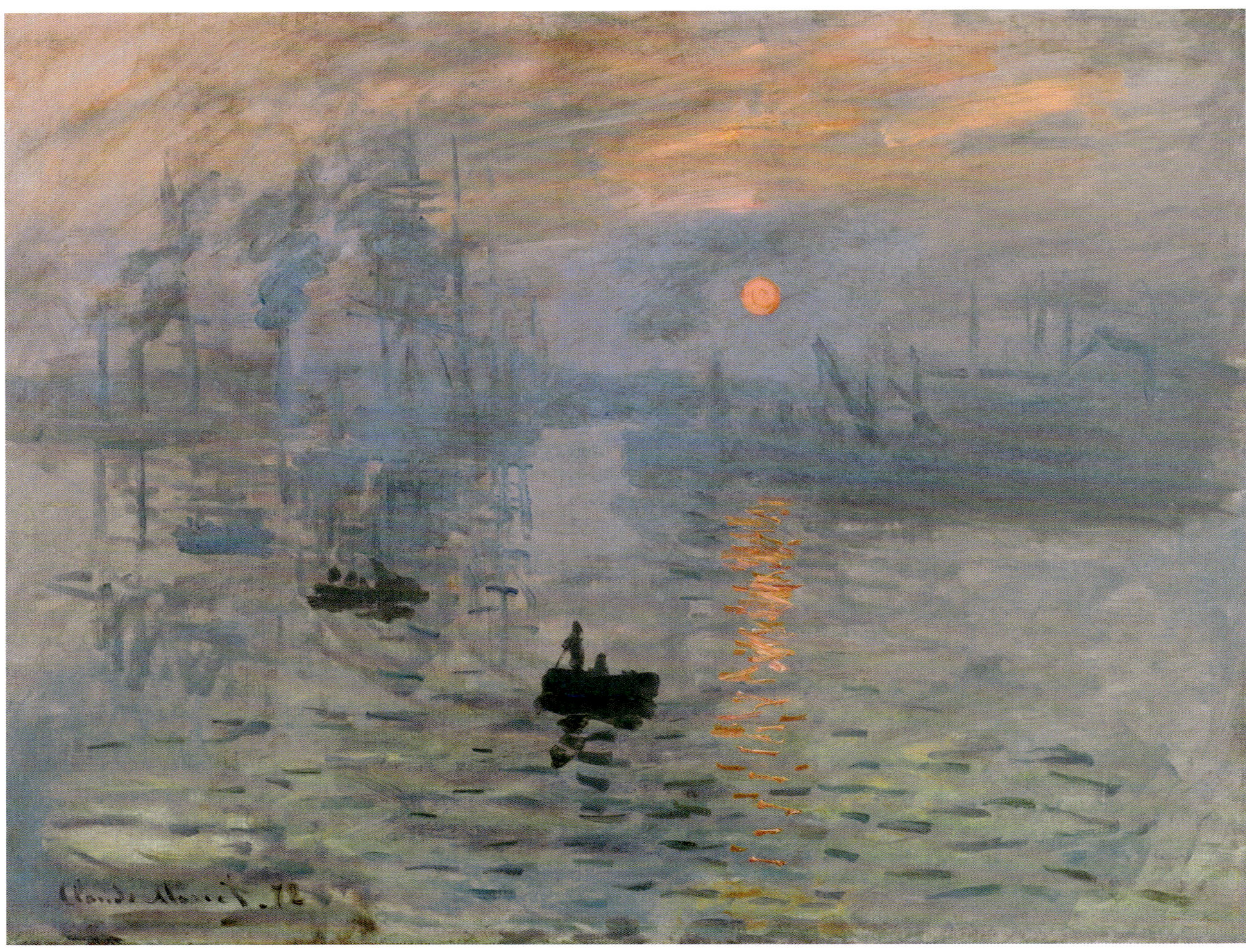

Seeing works such as Monet's *Impression, Sunrise* (fig. 1), the painting that inspired the derogatory term *Impressionism* when it was exhibited at the first show of the Anonymous Society of Painters, Sculptors, Printmakers, etc. in 1874, reproduced on coffee mugs and wall calendars is remarkable. It gives the impression that this kind of artwork was always in high demand, that it was always appreciated for its atmospheric effects, that its pastel hues were always seen as picturesque, that this art was beautiful enough to invite into our most intimate living spaces. And yet that couldn't be further from the truth.

Although today we use the term *Impressionist* to loosely describe the aesthetic of short, staccato strokes of bright pigments applied rapidly in one go, Impressionism as it emerged in the 1870s wasn't a style. Rather it was a collective of cutting-edge contemporary artists who banded together under a common cause: to find a way to make a living outside the conservative state-run fine arts system, because there was almost no support for their radical approach to painting, either in the press or from mainstream collectors. In fact, it was their rejection from the French government's official Salon exhibition—essentially the only path for professional success in nineteenth-century Paris—that drove them to organize their first group exhibition in 1874, following the model set by their mentors Gustave Courbet and Edouard Manet, both of whom had mounted private solo shows in 1867 on the grounds of the World's Fair in Paris.

Claude Monet, *Impression, Sunrise*, 1872. Oil on canvas. Musée Marmottan Monet.

To say that the artwork exhibited by the collective's founding members—Monet, Paul Cézanne, Pierre-Auguste Renoir, Degas, Alfred Sisley, Camille Pissarro, and Berthe Morisot—shocked the public is an understatement. A caricature produced by nineteenth-century French illustrator Cham in response to the collective's first show makes clear the revolutionary aspect of both the art and the act of mounting such an exhibition (fig. 2). The caption reads, "A revolution in painting and one that begins by causing terror," alluding not only to the French Revolution, but to the Reign of Terror, its most violent and destructive phase that was bent on destroying the vestiges of traditional French values.[1] The name Impressionism, which the group had begrudgingly accepted by 1877, was given to them by the French critic Louis Leroy as an insult in response to Monet's now iconic painting *Impression, Sunrise*: "*Impression*, of that I was sure. I also said to myself that, since I was impressed, there must be some impression in there. . . . And what freedom, what ease of brushwork! Wallpaper in its embryonic state is even more finished than this seascape."[2]

Over the course of the eight Impressionist exhibitions, which were organized between 1874 and 1886, critics and the public alike were utterly stunned by the cutting-edge contemporary art on display—but not in a good way. Among the most common criticisms launched at the group was that their paintings were garishly colored and horrifyingly ugly. Reviewing the third Impressionist show in 1877, the critic Bertall scoffed: "The majority of the time, they are awkward attempts, crude in color and tone, without contour and modeling, displaying the most complete disregard for drawing, distances and perspective; colors chucked, so to speak, at random, placed next to each other in flat tints with no blending. The search, most often, for

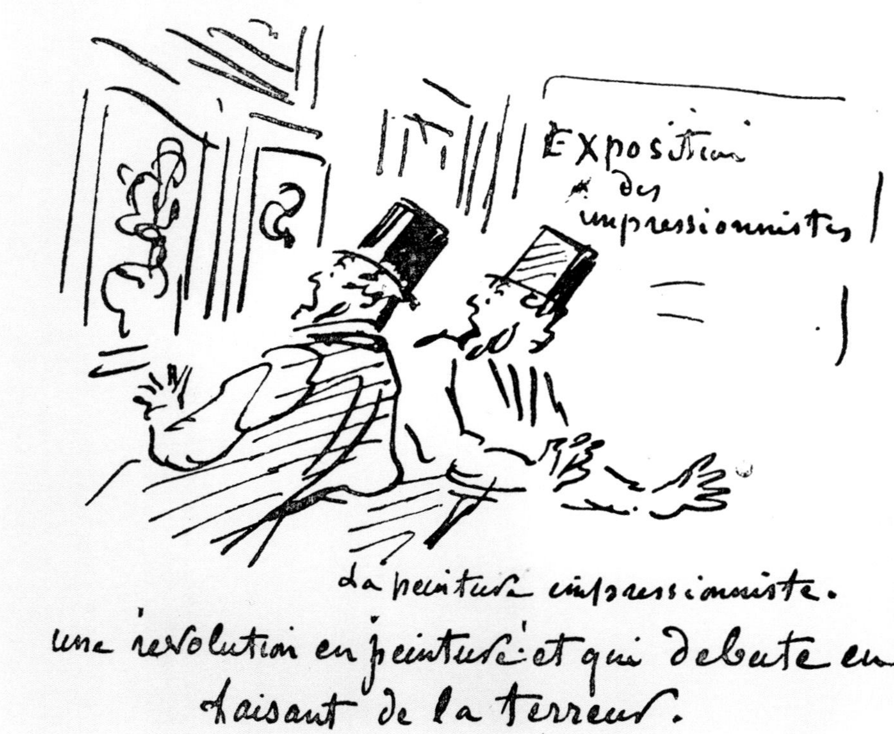

FIG. 2

Cham (Amédée Charles Henri de Noé), caricature of the first Impressionist Exhibition in Paris, 1874. Engraving. Bibliothèque Nationale, Paris, France.

13

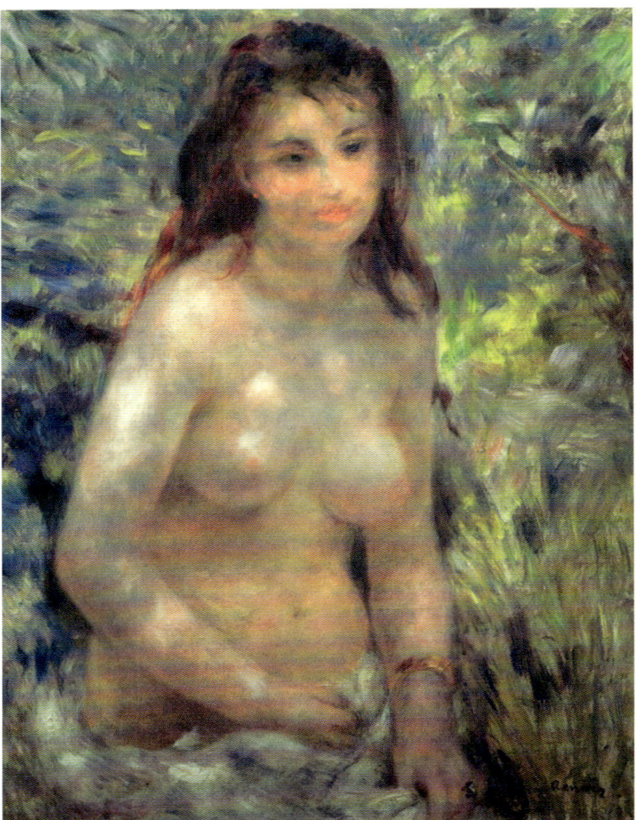

Pierre-Auguste Renoir,
Study. Torso, Sunlight Effect,
c. 1874. Oil on canvas.
Musée d'Orsay, Paris.

the grotesque and the ugly, to undoubtedly produce an impression of astonishment and surprise in the spectator […]."[3]

It can be hard today to understand why these paintings that so many find beautiful were seen as comical at best and grotesque at worst by the artists' contemporaries. Much of this was prompted by the bright pastel hues the Impressionists adopted to convey the optical sensation of light interacting with objects in the world around us. To represent nature not as we know it, but as we perceive it, the Impressionists rejected the Western Renaissance tradition that prioritized muted, naturalistic earth tones and the use of black in the depiction of three-dimensional volume and spatial recession. Touting that black rarely exists in nature in a pure state, they banished it from their depictions of depth and shadow, using instead shades of blue, violet, and green. Renoir's application of this technique caused an uproar at the second Impressionist show of 1876, when he exhibited *Study. Torso, Sunlight Effect,* his modern take on the time-honored tradition of

the female nude (fig. 3). Albert Wolff ranted in *Le Figaro*: "Try to explain to Mr. Renoir that a woman's torso is not a mass of decomposing flesh with the green and purplish blotches that indicate a state of complete putrefaction of the corpse!"[4] The complaint that the Impressionists' paintings, especially those by Gustave Caillebotte, were too blue or too violet became a constant refrain in the press. Reviewing the third Impressionist show, Bertall compared the overwhelming palette of blues and greens that he saw upon entering the gallery to Roquefort blue cheese.[5]

Whether positive or negative, the most frequent criticism aimed at the Impressionists, however, was their perceived inability to create a finished picture. One writer reviewing the 1877 show, where Monet's *The Gare Saint Lazare*, Renoir's *Ball at the Moulin de la Galette*, and Caillebotte's *The Pont de l'Europe* debuted, captured the critical zeitgeist: "The *impressionists* are painters who have the audacity to give us a glimpse, a simple impression of things, without making the effort to enter into the detailed study of line, of color, nor the thousand other knowing combinations that painters of the past had the good nature to be concerned with. A self-respecting *impressionist* (some say *impressionalist*) does not put on these airs and graces: he proceeds by the abrupt application of colors. He takes his brush and forcefully dabs the canvas; something shocking results from this process that stuns the viewer and it's our imagination that is responsible for completing [the picture]." He goes on to concede, "It's not that there aren't certain qualities in some of the works exhibited by the impressionists; but they are qualities of a very rudimentary nature: all of them made sketches, not one of them made a painting."[6]

Pierre-Auguste Renoir, *The Seine at Chatou*,
1874. Oil on canvas. Dallas Museum of Art, The
Wendy and Emery Reves Collection, 1985.R.62.

To understand this criticism, we must step back in time and consider what was at stake in the 1870s. A subset of the state-run Academy of Fine Arts, the Salon was the only non-commercial exhibition venue in Paris until the late nineteenth century. The primary purpose of this display of artwork was to educate the French public and elevate its morals through exposure to a strictly controlled set of aesthetic and philosophical values embodied by the artwork on view. To uphold this lofty ambition, the Academy appointed a jury that accepted or rejected submissions based on subject matter and style. Over the years, the rules changed regarding who was eligible to submit to the Salon or serve on its jury. Nevertheless, history paintings (those depicting religious, historic, or literary subjects) executed in a highly polished, illusionistic style were always championed by the Academy as the epitome of artistic achievement. The government rewarded those who adhered to the system with medals, commissions, and purchases for state collections.

The Impressionists turned their backs on the Academy's teachings and its exhibition system. They focused exclusively on mundane scenes drawn from middle-class life unfolding in and around Paris: the hustle and bustle of carriages and pedestrians on expansive boulevards (cats. 1, 2), quiet gardens and streets in Parisian suburbs (cats. 19–21, 23), sweeping views of coastal ports and major waterways (figs. 4, 5; cats. 11, 13–16), idyllic views of the countryside in France and beyond (cats. 18, 24–26), and serene still lifes in intimate domestic spaces (cats. 3–8). They worked rapidly, especially when painting outdoors, applying pigment wet-into-wet to capture their fleeting sensations before a motif. Polished brushwork

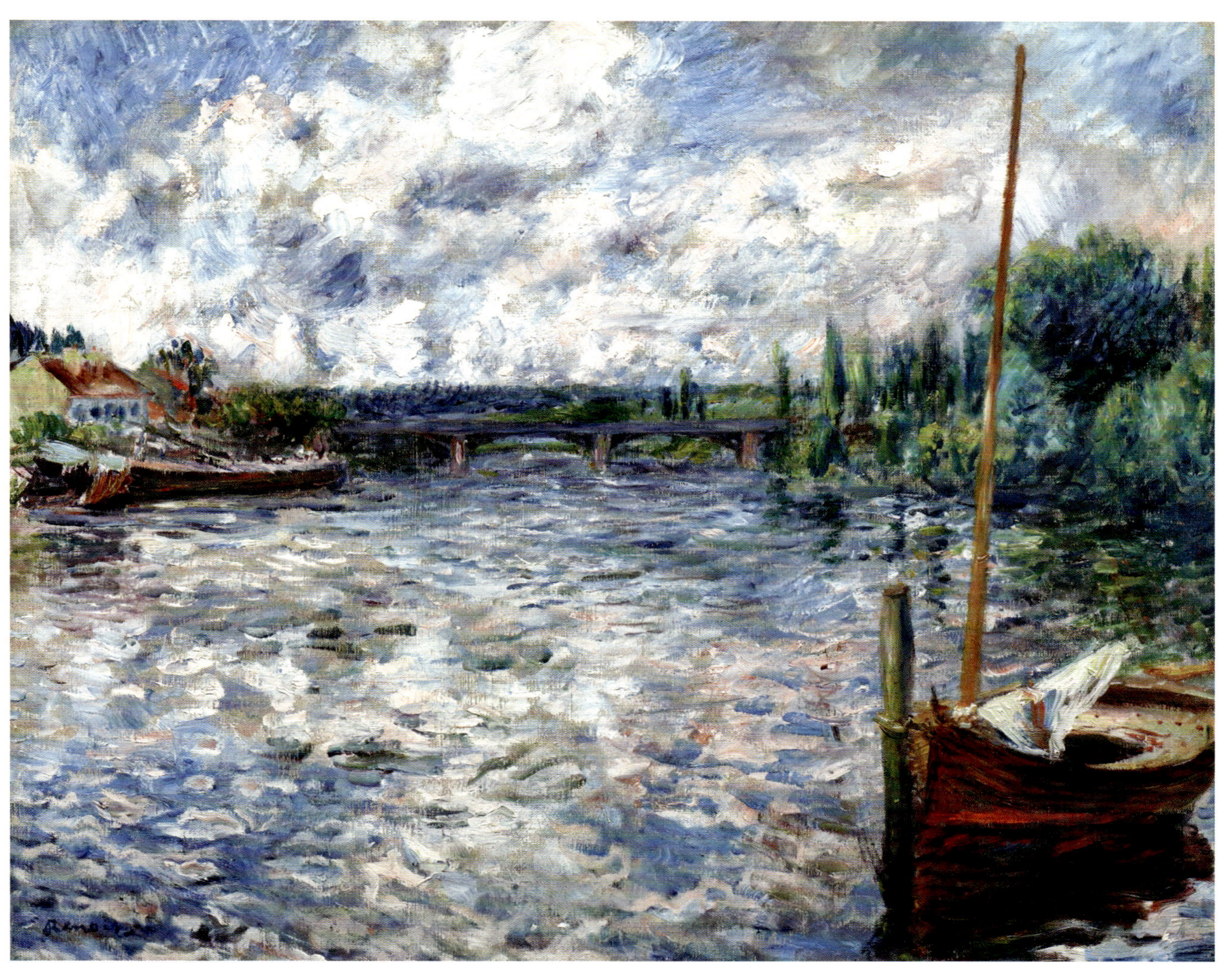

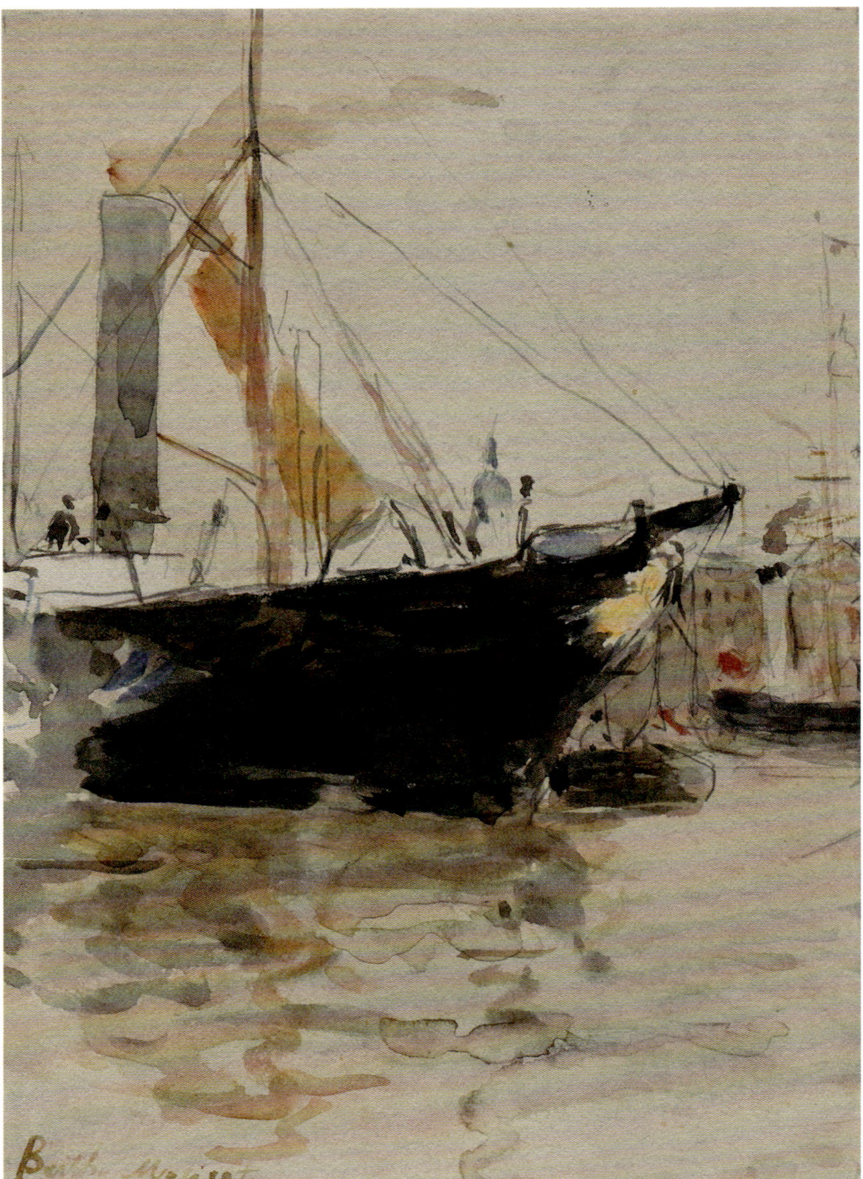

FIG. 5

Berthe Morisot, *Harbor Scene*, 1875 or 1882. Watercolor on paper. Dallas Museum of Art, bequest of William B. Jordan and Robert Dean Brownlee, 2019.72.39.

that eliminates the visible traces of the artist's hand was shunned in favor of loose, almost gestural dabs and dashes (cats. 20, 22, 27). Rather than illustrating space and form through line and volumetric shading, they constructed their compositions by layering and juxtaposing vibrant hues (cats. 12, 17, 26). They also abandoned the Academic technique of applying a brown preparatory wash to the canvas to serve as a midtone, as well as the thick topcoat of glossy varnish that signified a finished painting at the Salon. Instead, they applied paint directly to the light-colored ground or canvas to increase the colors' vibrancy, often leaving areas unpainted to enhance atmospheric or lighting effects (cat. 22).

The resulting effect of bright matte surfaces on which light sparkles, contours blur, and objects move in and out of focus was not only tolerated by the Academy and art critics but celebrated when observed in small oil sketches and studies. The latter were considered a preliminary step, however, and not the finished product. Professional painters were expected to use their intellect and imagination to transform these initial impressions into finished pictures in their studios—that is to say, into detailed and carefully composed paintings with invisible brushstrokes and naturalistic colors, the whole saturated with shiny varnish. By skirting the official Salon system and presenting what appeared to be sketches as finished paintings for public consumption, the Impressionists astounded both liberal and conservative visitors to their shows.

The press had a field day, with some contending that the art on view was an intentional joke made at the public's expense, while others felt it was an attack on the esteemed genre of painting itself. This act of challenging the state-sanctioned parameters on what constituted fine art and what was worthy of being shown to the public as fine art wasn't considered simply an audacious attack on French artistic values, but a subversive political act, so deeply were the two entwined in this period. By framing the Impressionist collective in this context, we can begin to understand how radical, challenging, and even offensive these paintings were to their contemporaries when exhibited between 1874 and 1886.

The Impressionists' rebellious insistence on depicting modern subjects in an equally modern style and displaying their works on their own terms was nothing short of a revolution. Its aftermath continues to reverberate not only in how art is made today, but also in how it's shared with the public. Impressionism is often held apart from the explosion of different modernisms that proliferated in the late nineteenth and early twentieth centuries. It can seem as if the Impressionists' most significant innovations— the bright, antinaturalistic palette, semi-abstract application of paint, and fixation on depicting the experience of modern living—ended in 1900, at which point the art world pivoted to something completely new. But of course, movements rarely unfold in straight lines from one to the next, following a neat chronology. A case in point: Monet, Degas, Renoir, and Mary Cassatt all continued to make artwork into

the opening decades of the twentieth century. They lived to see the development of new avant-garde styles such as Post-Impressionism (cats. 28, 29, 32, 35, 40, 41), Fauvism (cat. 43), Cubism, Expressionism (cats. 44, 46, 47), and Abstraction (cat. 45), whose roots stem from the revolution they started with their cohort nearly fifty years prior.

The Impressionist exhibitions were generally considered to have been a critical and financial failure, with few artists finding buyers for their challenging contemporary art. Those who eventually earned recognition and success didn't do so until after the last group show was held in 1886. But the story of Impressionism isn't simply about the artists who participated in the exhibitions or adopted its radical aesthetic. It's also about the long shadow the movement cast that dwarfed successive generations of would-be avant-garde artists. Paul Gauguin, Vincent van Gogh, Pierre Bonnard, Henri Matisse, Piet Mondrian, Edvard Munch, and Ernst Kirchner, among many others, grappled with its legacy, whether adapting or reacting against its core tenets in their quest to plot the trajectory of modern art. Even today, when we see artwork in museums and galleries that reflects our collective lived experience— unremarkable domestic moments, snapshots of life in urban and rural settings, assemblages made from the detritus of contemporary life, abstract compositions that declare the primacy of color and mark making to convey a mood, sensation, or impression—we can credit the Impressionists for having the audacity to start this revolutionary war, even if they themselves lost the battle.

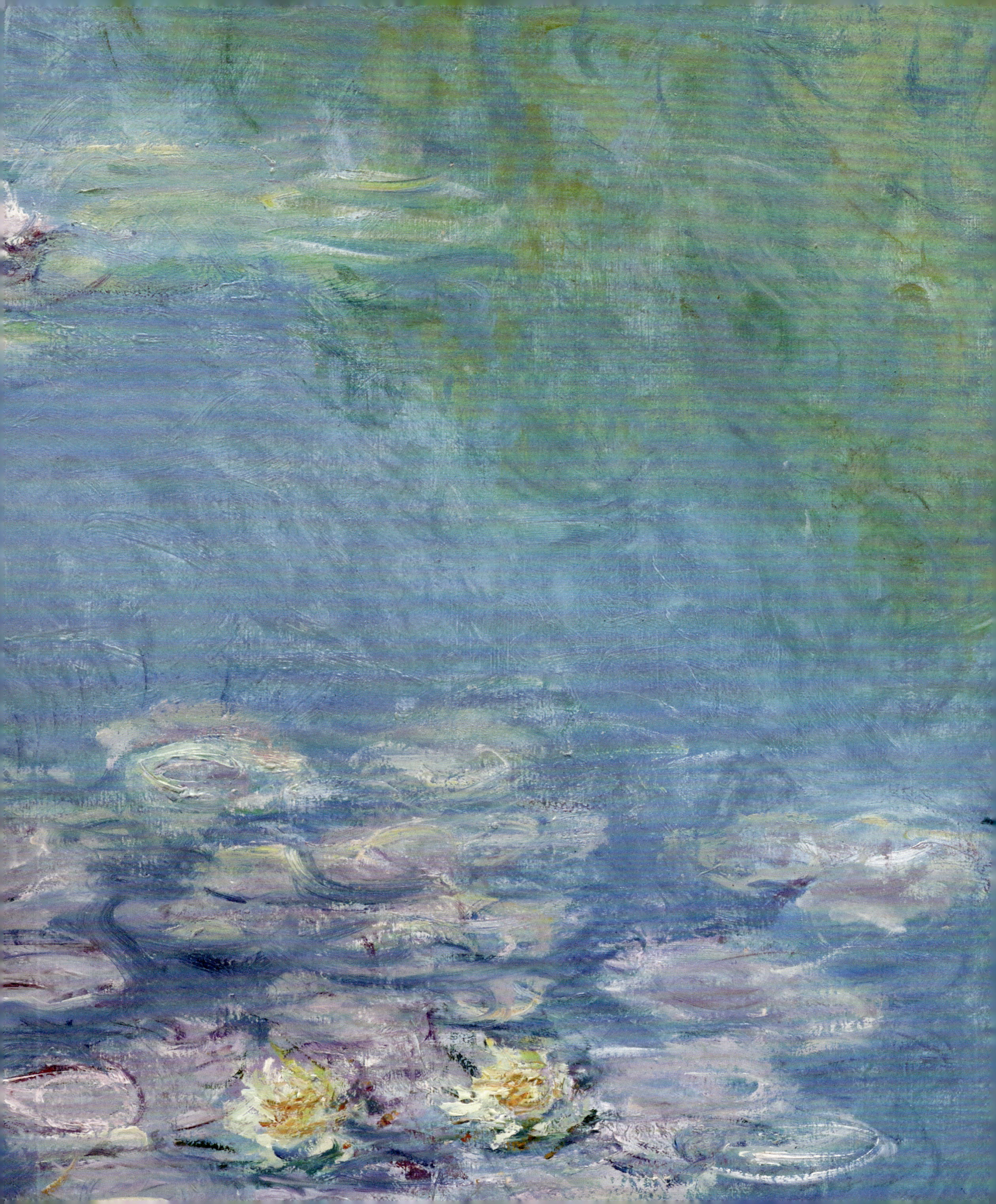

Monet to Matisse

AT THE DALLAS MUSEUM OF ART

Nicole R. Myers

The Impressionist Revolution: Monet to Matisse from the Dallas Museum of Art traces the rebellious origins of the independent artist collective known as the Impressionists and follows the revolutionary course they set for modern art. Breaking with tradition in both how and what they painted, as well as how they showed their work, the Impressionists redefined what constituted cutting-edge contemporary art. The unique innovations of its core members—Gustave Caillebotte, Mary Cassatt, Paul Cézanne, Edgar Degas, Claude Monet, Berthe Morisot, Camille Pissarro, Pierre-Auguste Renoir, and Alfred Sisley—set the foundation against which following generations of avant-garde artists reacted, from Paul Gauguin and Vincent van Gogh to Piet Mondrian and Henri Matisse.[1] That the Impressionists' legacy can be told entirely through the Dallas Museum of Art's exceptional holdings is a testament to the continued commitment of the Museum and its greatest benefactors to build one of the premier collections of this material in the country.

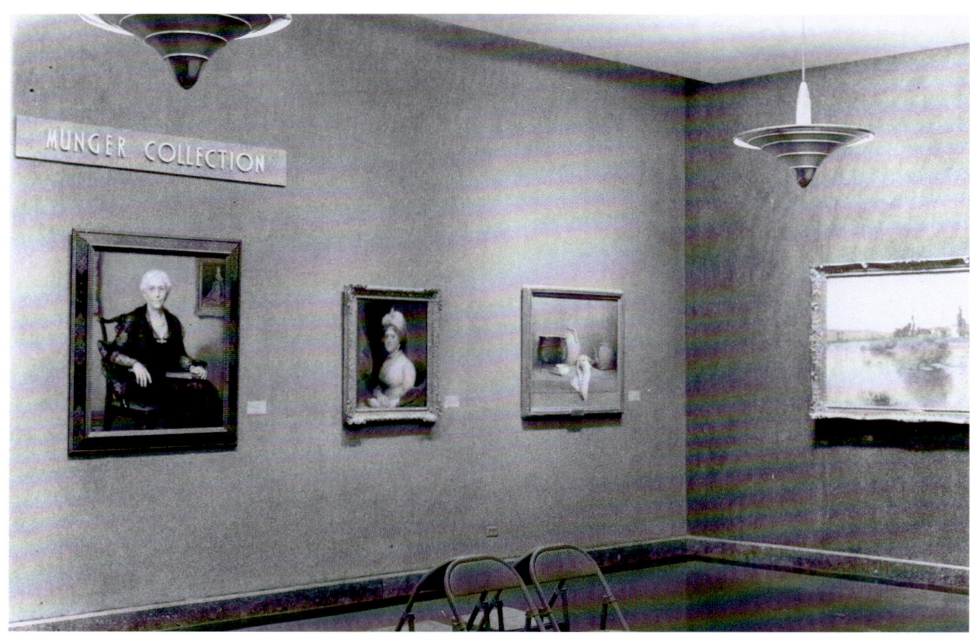

FIG. 6

Claude Monet's *The Seine at Lavacourt* installed in the Munger Collection gallery at the DMA's Fair Park location. Date unknown.

Americans have had a long love affair with Impressionism, longer in fact than the French, whose culture birthed this groundbreaking movement. Our relatively young country didn't have its own deep-rooted art tradition or government-sanctioned art school that set the tone for what was and wasn't considered important art. The result was a more open-minded attitude toward contemporary art production that started first with private individuals in the mid-1880s and then moved quickly to public art institutions. From coast to coast, encyclopedic museums in the U.S. display an overwhelming preference for Impressionist and Post-Impressionist paintings in their galleries. In this regard, the DMA is no different. Yet beyond its enviable quality and breadth, the DMA's collection is distinguished by how recently it was formed. Unlike most of its American peers, whose core collections were formed in the first half of the twentieth century, the DMA acquired its Impressionist and Post-Impressionist paintings, pastels, and works on paper in the last thirty years, thanks to some of the most staggering acts of philanthropy this city has seen.

Founded in 1903, the Dallas Museum of Art had humble beginnings, opening its first gallery as the Dallas Art Association in the new Dallas Public Library.

Over the ensuing decades, the Museum changed its name and location several times, in addition to expanding its scope to encompass works ranging from antiquity to the art of today. But something that never changed was its commitment to building a global collection of artwork from all cultures, periods, and media in order to bring the best of human creativity to all who walk through its doors, whether physical or digital. The DMA's collection, which today stands at about 26,000 objects and counting, reflects the passion and generosity of thousands of private individuals and foundations that donated artwork and acquisition funds. Indeed, the Impressionist collection began with two exceptional purchases made by the Mrs. Stephen I. Munger Trust, which was founded in 1925 to purchase art for the fledgling museum.

From its first European acquisition in 1937 to its last in 2016, the Munger Fund amassed eight important examples of painting and sculpture that represent the height of artistic achievement from the Gothic period through Impressionism. Viewed together, the works reflect the Munger Fund's founding mission to acquire the best, most representative examples of art from varying times and places using the utmost discernment. The impressive acquisition of Claude

Monet's *The Seine at Lavacourt* in 1938—the second purchase made by the fund—simultaneously brought the first Monet and the first example of French Impressionism to the Museum (cat. 16, fig. 6).

Grand in format and scale, *The Seine at Lavacourt* is one of the rare paintings that Monet produced for submission to the Paris Salon during the run of the Impressionist exhibitions between 1874 and 1886. It was based on sketches that he made during a harsh winter spell that froze the River Seine and many of its branches (fig. 7). From his floating studio boat, Monet raced to capture the unusual sight of the ice as it melted and broke apart. Back in his studio, he used the small studies painted en plein air to create large showpieces whose stable compositions and more polished brushwork were intended to appease the conservative Salon jury. Monet submitted to the jury both *The Seine at Lavacourt*, reimagined as a summer scene, and an identically scaled view of the ice floes at dusk. Of the two, only *The Seine at Lavacourt* was accepted for exhibition. Monet's hopes of securing a clientele and financial stability were dashed, however, when the canvas did not attract much attention. He never attempted to exhibit at the Salon again. Nevertheless, with its emphasis on light reflecting off water, *The Seine at Lavacourt* spectacularly anticipates

the series of water lily paintings that would eventually, in the last twenty years of his life, earn Monet the financial and critical success he sought.

The Seine at Lavacourt set the tone for the Munger Fund's dedication to collecting cutting-edge examples of nineteenth-century French painting. Cassatt's *Sleepy Baby*, a brilliantly hued oil pastel that demonstrates both the medium and subject matter for which the artist is celebrated, was acquired in 1952. This was followed in both significance and visual appeal by the 1955 acquisition of Camille Pissarro's *Apple Harvest* (cat. 26), a dazzling example of the Pointillist technique pioneered by Georges Seurat. These three masterpieces founded the core of the DMA's Impressionist collection. To this day, the Munger Fund Monet and Pissarro are among the Museum's most iconic and frequently requested works for loan.

The 1960s saw renewed interest in acquiring Impressionist and Post-Impressionist paintings. Through the generosity of Dallas collectors and foundations, a handful of phenomenal paintings came into the collection one after the next. Eugene and Margaret McDermott, the DMA's single greatest benefactors, gifted Van Gogh's *River Bank in Springtime* in memory of their friend Arthur Berger in 1961 (fig. 8).

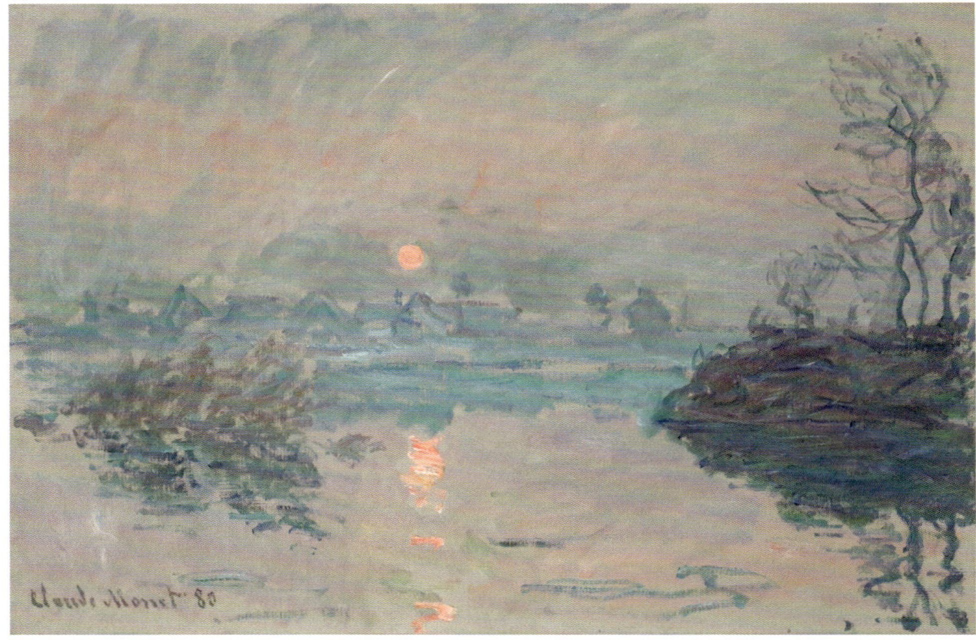

FIG. 7

Claude Monet, *Seine at Lavacourt, Winter Effect*, 1880. Oil on canvas. Private collection.

The Foundation for the Arts, a Dallas-based nonprofit organization whose mission is to acquire eighteenth- and nineteenth-century artwork for the benefit of the Museum, purchased Gauguin's *I Raro te Oviri (Under the Pandanus)* (cat. 28) in 1963, the year of the foundation's inception. Despite this strong start, however, these paintings remained relatively isolated in the DMA's collection for nearly three decades. It was only in the early 1980s that the Museum's holdings of Impressionism and Post-Impressionism—which at this point were represented by about ten paintings—were rapidly transformed through two significant gifts.

The first came in 1981 through the benevolence of The Meadows Foundation, which made an extraordinary gift of thirty-eight Impressionist, modern, and contemporary paintings and sculptures collected by the late Algur H. Meadows with his wife, Virginia. Among the historic European paintings gifted from the couple's personal collection were *Valle Buona, Near Bordighera* and *Water Lilies* by Monet (cats. 17, 20), *Peasant Woman Carrying Two Bundles of Hay* by Pissarro (cat. 24), *Interior (Madame Vuillard and Grandmother Roussel at L'Étang-la-Ville)* by the Nabis painter Edouard Vuillard (fig. 9), *Nude, Yellow Background* by Pierre Bonnard (cat. 49), and Morisot's *Winter* (fig. 10), the first example by this founding Impressionist to enter the DMA's collection. A rarity in Morisot's body of work, *Winter* features an elegant and stylish woman—a type known as *la Parisienne* that was Morisot's specialty—as a personification of the season. *Winter* and *Summer* (Musée Fabre, Montpellier, France), its pendant, were shown to great critical acclaim at the fifth Impressionist exhibition in 1880. The critic Paul-Armand Silvestre admired *Winter* "with its figure, so courageously modern, of the Parisian woman braving the cold in her furs."[2]

The second major gift came just three years later, when Wendy Reves donated the staggering collection of 950 paintings, pastels, sculptures, and decorative art objects that she and her late husband, Emery, had purchased to decorate their villa in southern France. Among the gift are eighty-seven exemplary paintings and works on paper that serve as a "who's who" of French avant-garde artists of the nineteenth

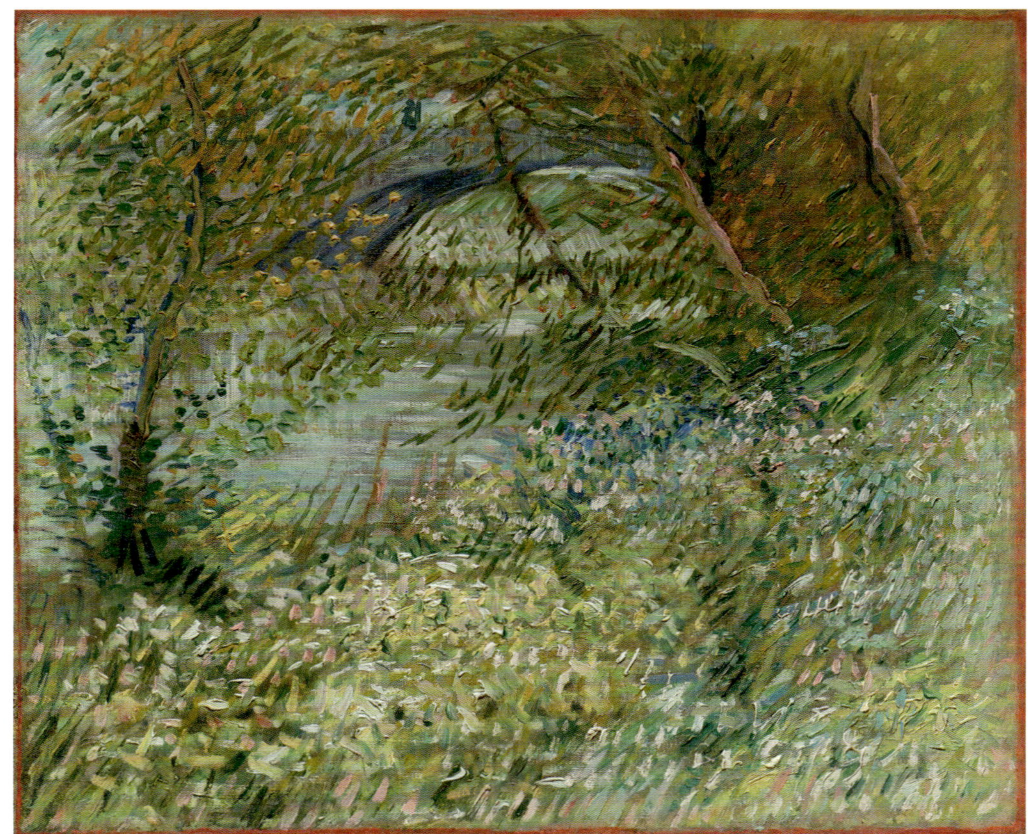

FIG. 8

Vincent van Gogh, *River Bank in Springtime*, 1887. Oil on canvas. Dallas Museum of Art, gift of Mr. and Mrs. Eugene McDermott in memory of Arthur Berger, 1961.99.

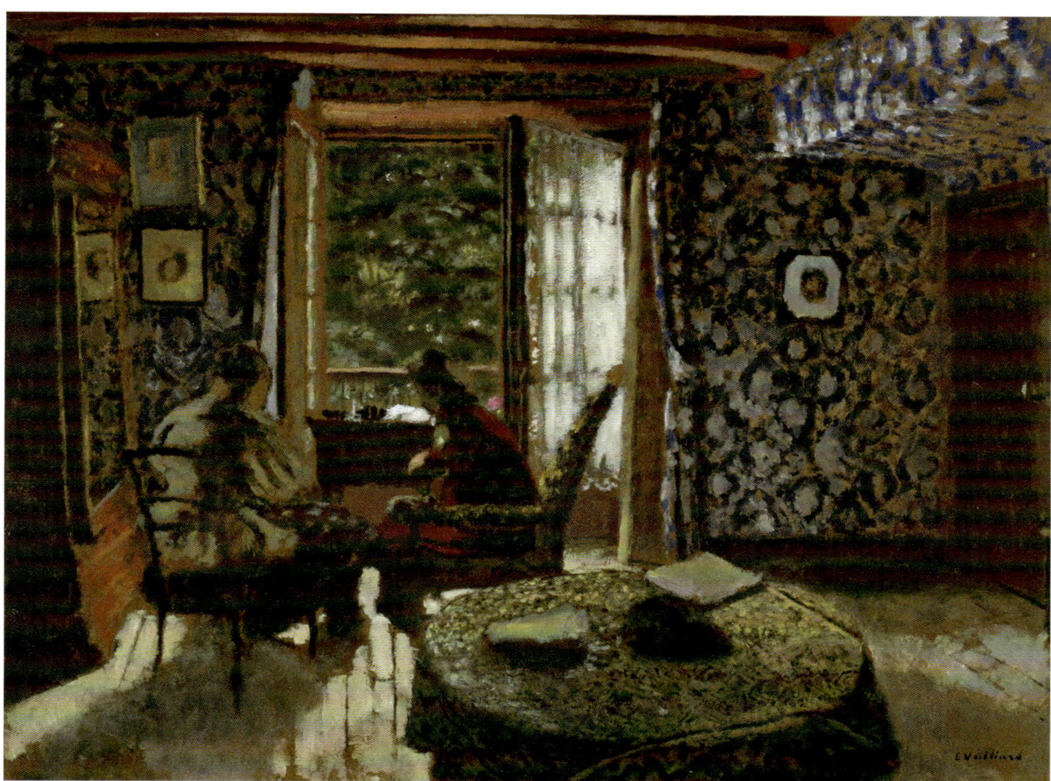

FIG. 9

Edouard Vuillard, *Interior (Madame Vuillard and Grandmother Roussel at L'Étang-la-Ville)*, c. 1902. Oil on cardboard. Dallas Museum of Art, gift of the Meadows Foundation, Incorporated, 1981.137.

and twentieth centuries: Bonnard, Cézanne, Gustave Courbet, Degas, Gauguin, Edouard Manet, Monet, Morisot, Pissarro, Renoir, Seurat, Sisley, Henri de Toulouse-Lautrec, Maurice de Vlaminck, Vuillard, Van Gogh, and Odilon Redon. In addition to its high quality and breadth, the Reves collection is also notable for its depth of representation. Several artists are represented by multiple examples in diverse media; for example, the Reves gift didn't only give the Museum its first works by Renoir and Cézanne, it gave eight remarkable paintings and drawings by Renoir and three oil and watercolor paintings by Cézanne.

Pastels and works on paper by Degas, Toulouse-Lautrec, Redon, and Van Gogh are among the great strengths of the collection, as are early examples of Impressionism by its founding members. Painted in 1871, Monet's *The Pont Neuf* (cat. 1) conjures the sensation of street life in Paris on a gray and windy day. Gestural, rapidly applied strokes of paint emphasize the movement of pedestrians, horse-drawn carriages, and steamboats, their blurry, unfinished forms conveying both movement and the physical sensation of rain and wind. Images like this one of

city life captured in oil paint with a loose, sketchy style were a novelty in 1870s France. Rebelling against the naturalistic style and more timeless, picturesque subjects favored by art critics and collectors of the time, Monet developed an approach that would come to define the Impressionist movement he helped launch just a few years later.

Cézanne's *Still Life with Carafe, Milk Can, Bowl, and Orange* (cat. 7) reflects a critical moment in the artist's development of a unique method for depicting space. Moving away from the bright, thickly applied colors of his early works and those of his peers, Cézanne deployed small parallel brushstrokes of muted colors to construct the essential shape and mass of each object in the still life. This innovative treatment of painting two-dimensional objects like wallpaper in the same manner as a three-dimensional object like an orange, of reducing objects to their most basic geometric forms, of merging foreground with background, challenges the viewer's logical understanding of depth and volume and planted the seeds for the Cubist style developed by Pablo Picasso and Georges Braque at the turn of the century.

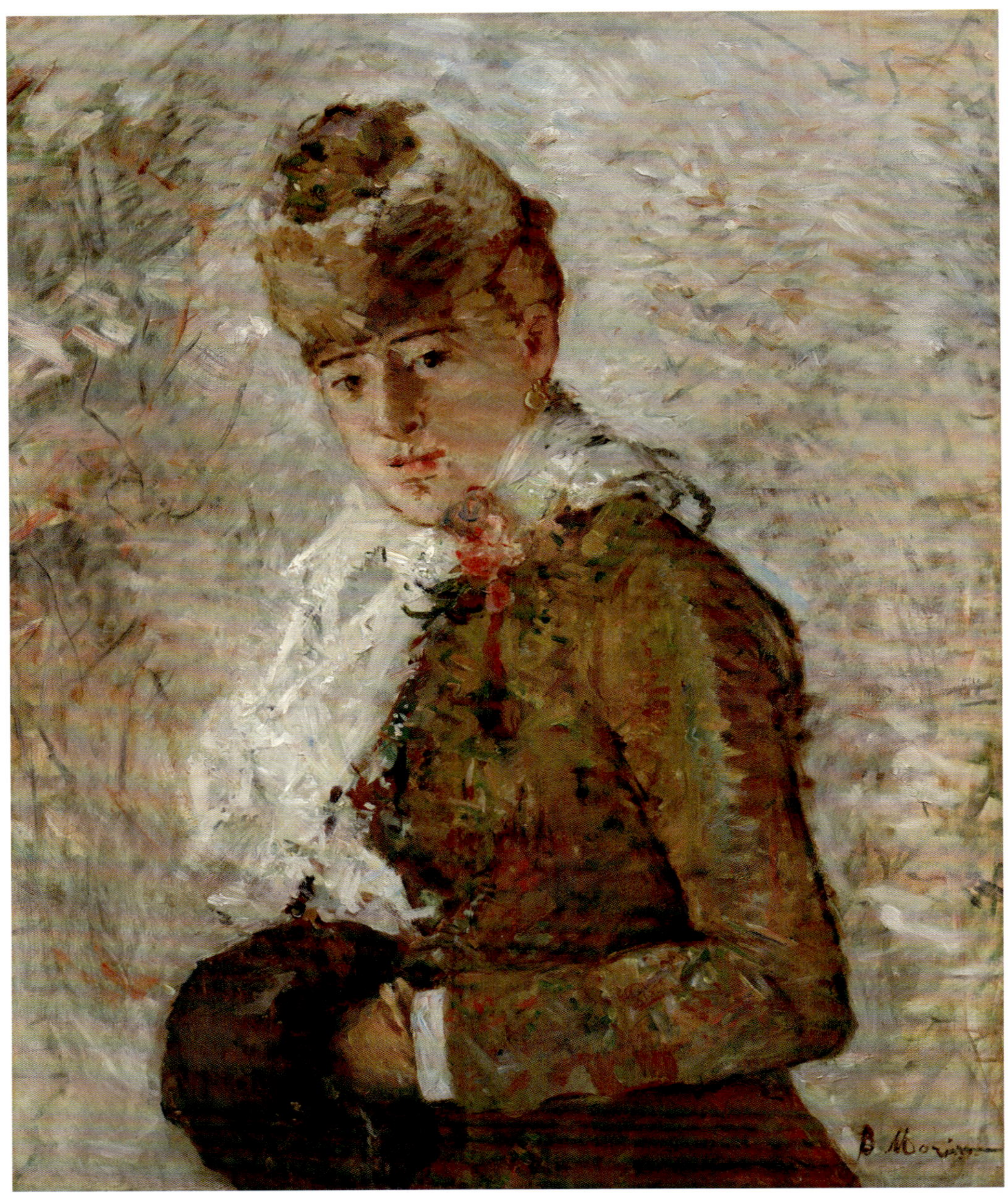

FIG. 10

Berthe Morisot, *Winter*, 1881. Oil on canvas. Dallas Museum of Art, gift of the Meadows Foundation, Incorporated, 1981.129.

The generosity of Wendy and Emery Reves marked a turning point. After this staggering gift, the DMA's collection of Impressionist and Post-Impressionist art expanded exponentially. Over the next thirty years, gifts by local art collectors and purchases by Dallas-based organizations bolstered the growing collection. Working closely with the Museum's curators, the Foundation for the Arts continued to purchase significant examples of Post-Impressionism, including Félix Vallotton's *The Laundress, Blue Room* (cat. 37) and Louis Anquetin's *Woman at Her Toilette* (cat. 30), in addition to augmenting the DMA's

holdings by accepting countless gifts, among them Paul Sérusier's *Celtic Tale* (cat. 35) from Frederick and Mildred Mayer, and nine sensational paintings by Piet Mondrian from James and Lillian Clark. The latter trace the artist's evolution from experimenting with Impressionist and Post-Impressionist techniques to the groundbreaking geometric abstractions for which he is best known today (cats. 39, 42).

Like the Foundation for the Arts, The Eugene and Margaret McDermott Art Fund, Inc., was established with the singular purpose of helping the DMA build a world-class collection, especially its holdings of non-

Western art, European painting and sculpture, and decorative arts. In the six decades since its inception, the McDermott Art Fund acquired more than three thousand objects from around the world that span all time periods, cultures, and media. In the area of nineteenth- and twentieth-century European art, it made possible the acquisition of many firsts to enter the Museum's collection, such as the first sculpture by Degas (cat. 10) and the first paintings by Caillebotte, Paul Signac, and Matisse (cats. 5, 25, 50). Nevertheless, it was the McDermotts' final act of generosity that cemented the DMA's collection of Impressionist and Post-Impressionist art as one of the best in the country. With Margaret's passing in 2018, the McDermott Art Fund was bequeathed thirty-two Impressionist and modernist masterpieces from the couple's personal collection. Between 1963 and 1993, Eugene and Margaret acquired masterpiece after masterpiece, filling their home with exceptional paintings and sculptures by Eugène Boudin, Caillebotte, Cézanne, Degas, Monet, Edvard Munch, Pissarro, Renoir, Sisley, and Signac, to name but a few.

Among the many treasures of the McDermott collection are three paintings by Monet that not only doubled the Museum's holdings by this founding member of Impressionism, but also introduced new subjects and time periods from the artist's spectacular career. Although primarily known for his landscapes, Monet was also a prodigious still-life painter, especially during his early career. Painted in 1872, *Still Life, Tea Service* (cat. 3) demonstrates Monet's remarkable ability to conjure a variety of different textures using a limited palette and evocative brushwork. The velvety sage leaves contrast with the matte tablecloth, the slick red lacquered tray, the shine of the blue-and-white china, and the reflections on a silver spoon. *Still Life, Tea Service* was included in the first exhibition of Impressionist paintings held in New York City in 1886.

Monet's *Poplars, Pink Effect* (cat. 18) belongs to a series of twenty-four paintings that depict a line of poplar trees planted along a river. As with his other serial paintings, such as those portraying haystacks or the Rouen Cathedral, Monet returned to the motif day after day, recording its appearance at different times and in varying light and weather conditions. *Poplars, Pink Effect* marks the first work from Monet's production in the 1890s to enter the DMA's collection, and visitors can now explore works from each decade of his long career, from 1870 to 1910.

Another example of Monet's serial production is *The Water Lily Pond (Clouds)* (cat. 19), one of more than 250 paintings of the artist's water garden that were produced during the last twenty years of his life. While the early pictures look out across the water and feature glimpses of sky, architectural elements, and the surrounding landscape, Monet eventually abandoned solid ground, shifting his viewpoint down and creating immersive, almost abstract images of the water's surface, as is the case with the Meadows water lilies from 1908 (cat. 20). The McDermott painting lands somewhere in between Monet's starting and end points within the series. Any indication of the sky has been eliminated, and our field of vision is almost entirely occupied by reflections mirrored on the pond's surface. Yet the inclusion of a grassy bank and overhanging foliage along the very top of the composition reveals that Monet had not yet moved away from the more traditional practice of situating the viewer in the landscape. Painted five years apart, the DMA's two water lilies capture a specific moment in Monet's evolution from realism to abstraction.

In addition to the Monets, the McDermott bequest brought other firsts to the collection, such as the first painting by André Derain. Painted in Provence in the summer of 1906, *Fishing Boats at L'Estaque* (cat. 43) demonstrates the hallmarks of Fauvism, the innovative style inspired by Seurat's Pointillism and developed by Derain and Matisse the year before. Against large areas of unpainted canvas, Derain placed boats, fishermen, a dock, and distant mountains in confident, unwavering strokes of solid reds, yellows, pinks, greens, and blues arranged like pieces of a puzzle. The exposed white ground signifies light reflecting off sky and water, a lesson passed down from Impressionists such as Renoir and Morisot.

Munch's *Thuringian Forest* (cat. 47), which greeted visitors when they entered the McDermotts' home, is the first oil painting by this modern master to join the

DMA's galleries. Munch encountered the Thuringian Forest in Germany while recuperating from alcohol-related health problems in the nearby sanatorium at Bad Elgersburg. Devoid of human figures, the undulating landscape is rendered as bleeding and raw, with sinuous pink and red strokes of paint contrasting with complementary hues of greens. Inspired by the works of Van Gogh and Gauguin, Munch developed a unique Expressionist style in which exaggerated colors and brushstrokes convey the artist's emotions of tension, anguish, and despair.

The Impressionist Revolution doesn't only tell the legacy of collecting Impressionism and Post-Impressionism at the DMA, however, nor is it a thing of the past. The Museum's commitment to bringing the finest examples to Dallas is shared by local collectors, such as the Pauline Allen Gill Foundation. The latter's impressive collection includes several stunning Impressionist and Post-Impressionist paintings by Cassatt, Pissarro, and Sisley, among others, that have been generously lent to the DMA since 2006. And in 2023, Ralph and Cornelia Heins completed a gift of a group of thirty paintings, sculptures, and works on paper that Marie "Elinor" Heins formed in Montreux, Switzerland, between 1967 and her death in 2018. Like the McDermott bequest, the Heins collection is divided evenly between late nineteenth- and early twentieth-century art movements: Impressionism, Post-Impressionism, and German Expressionism, Elinor's favorite. The gift includes works by Boudin, Renoir, Signac, Sisley, Toulouse-Lautrec, Kirchner, Alexei Jawlensky, and a rare Munch. The latter's *View from Hisøya Near Arendal* (cat. 38) reveals the stylistic exploration that defined the artist's early career as he experimented with Impressionism in search of a personal style.

Another standout work in the Heins collection is Alexei Jawlensky's vibrant depiction of the town of Murnau in the foothills of the Bavarian Alps (cat. 46). The picture dates from a summer of whirlwind artistic activity while Jawlensky was in the company of fellow avant-garde painters such as Wassily Kandinsky (fig. 11) and Gabriele Münter. Painted in the crucial years leading up to their founding of the Blue Rider group, the artists' landscapes produced in Murnau reveal the influence of Post-Impressionism and Fauvism while foreshadowing the importance of color in conveying spiritual value central to the early Expressionists. With the Heins gift, particularly its Expressionist works, the DMA can now tell a more complete story of Impressionism's legacy, which crossed time and space in the artistic cauldron that simmered in Europe in the run up to the Second World War.

The Impressionist Revolution: Monet to Matisse from the Dallas Museum of Art thus weaves together two revolutionary stories. One recounts the pioneering origins of the Impressionist collective and the legacy of its founding members on the development of the most significant modern art movements in Europe in the first half of the twentieth century. The other, more subtle narrative is the legacy of the passionate collectors and tireless patrons who built the DMA's world-class collection in a record amount of time. It is often said in Texas "go big or go home." This bold and daring spirit is perfectly aligned with the extraordinary collection of Impressionism, Post-Impressionism, and early modernism that these visionary philanthropists gifted to the people of Dallas and beyond.

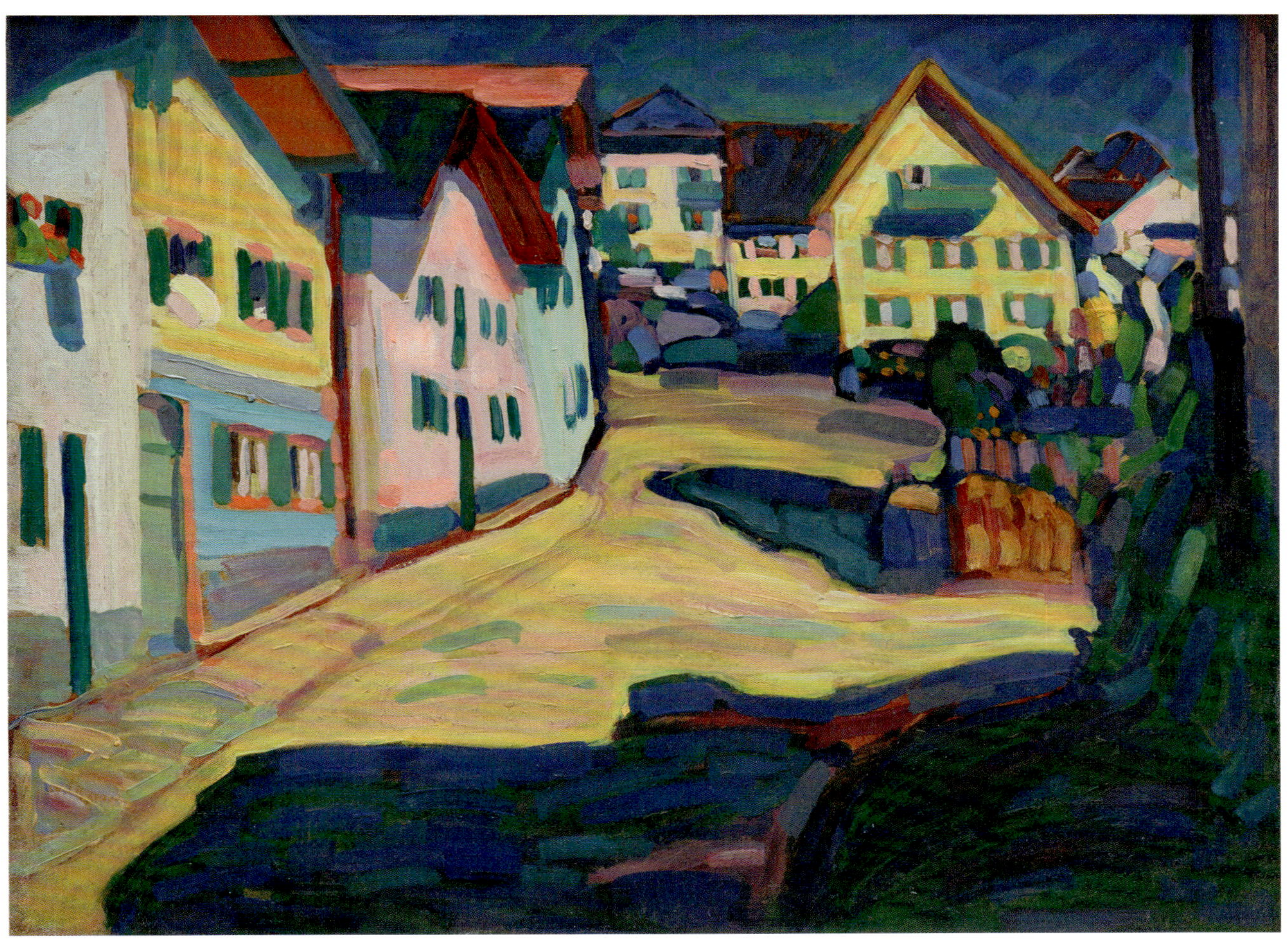

FIG. 11

Wassily Kandinsky, *Murnau, Burggrabenstrasse 1, 1908*,
1908. Oil on paper mounted on Masonite.
Dallas Museum of Art, Dallas Art Association
Purchase, 1963.31.

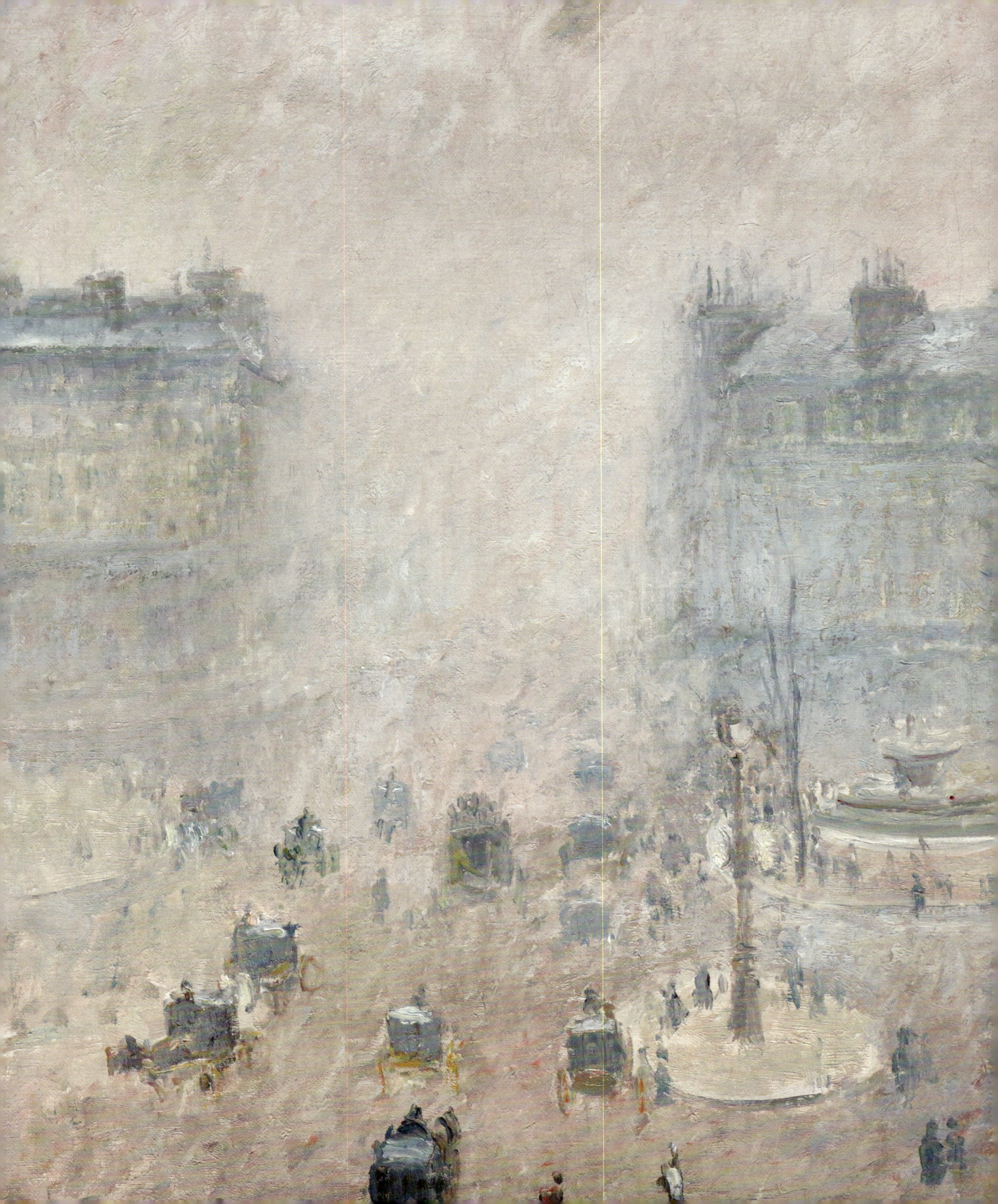

Rebels with a Cause

IN 1874, an artist's collective that called itself the Anonymous Society of Painters, Sculptors, Printmakers, etc. opened the first of what would become eight group shows held over the course of twelve years. The participants in each exhibition varied, and, beyond a shared rejection of artistic tradition, so did their subjects and approaches. What unified these independent artists we now call the Impressionists was the desire to publicly exhibit their work. By mounting their own exhibitions, this collective bypassed the official Salon organized by the state-run Academy of Fine Arts, an act that was as rebellious as it was entrepreneurial.

In contrast to the historical subjects and traditional styles championed by the Academy, the Impressionists shared a passion for capturing everyday modern life in all its realities, from the spectacular to the mundane, in an equally modern style. The industrialization that was rapidly changing both city and country provided the Impressionists with endless inspiration, as did the growing middle class it spawned. Speeding carriages, iron bridges, and steam-powered transportation punctuate Parisian vistas and verdant fields. Intimate scenes of bourgeois domesticity, leisure activities, and urban entertainment are elevated to the status of high art. Even the time-honored tradition of the classical nude was subverted into a modern bather.

Despite the artists' efforts, the Impressionist exhibitions scandalized the Parisian public and were generally considered a failure. Apart from a few forward-thinking critics and collectors, there was little appreciation or market for their subversive artwork until well after their last show in 1886.

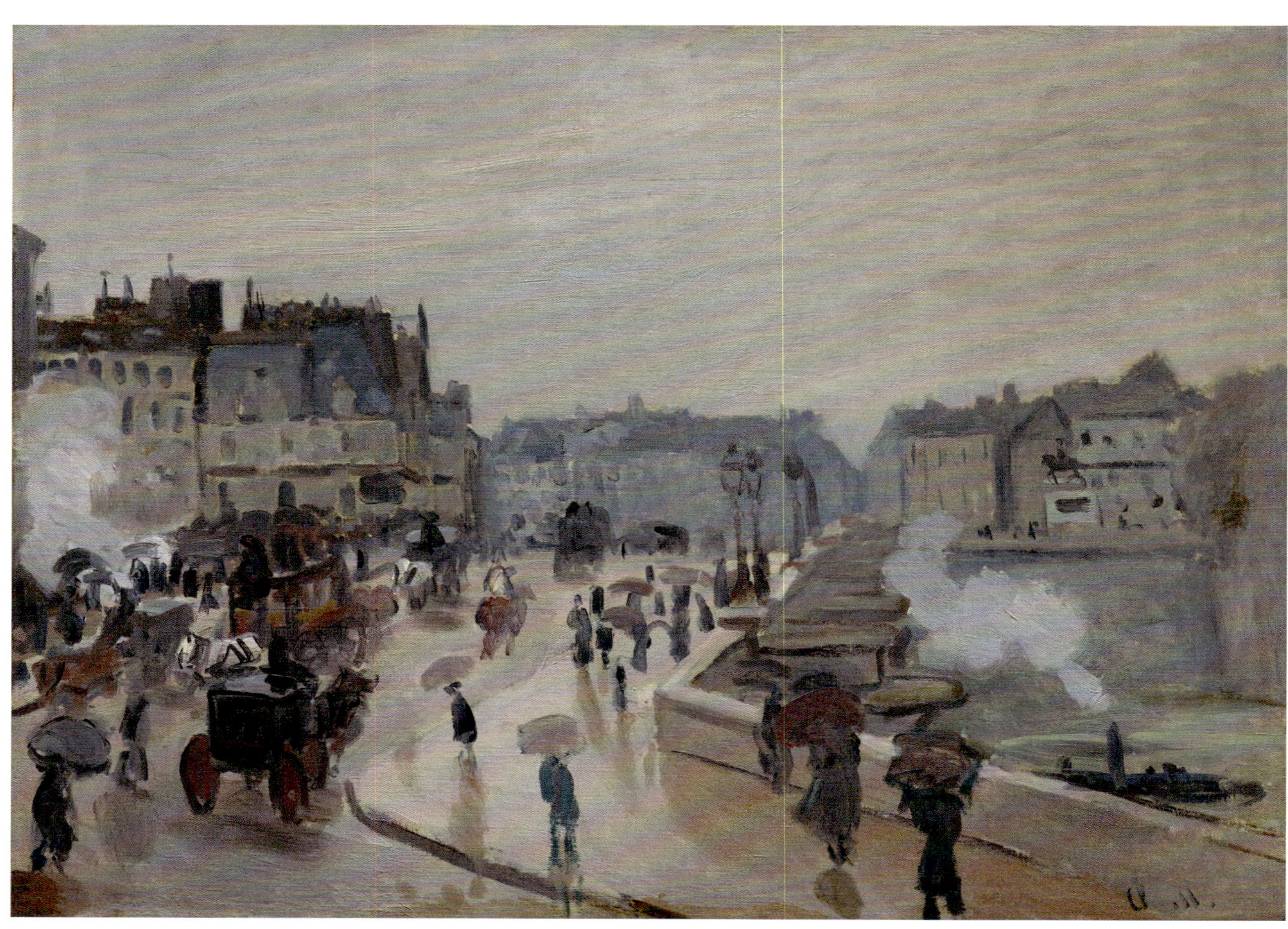

CAT. 1

Claude Monet
(born in Paris, France, 1840–died in Giverny, France, 1926)
The Pont Neuf
1871
Oil on canvas, 21 × 28 ¾ in. (53.3 × 73.0 cm)
Dallas Museum of Art, The Wendy and Emery Reves Collection, 1985.R.38

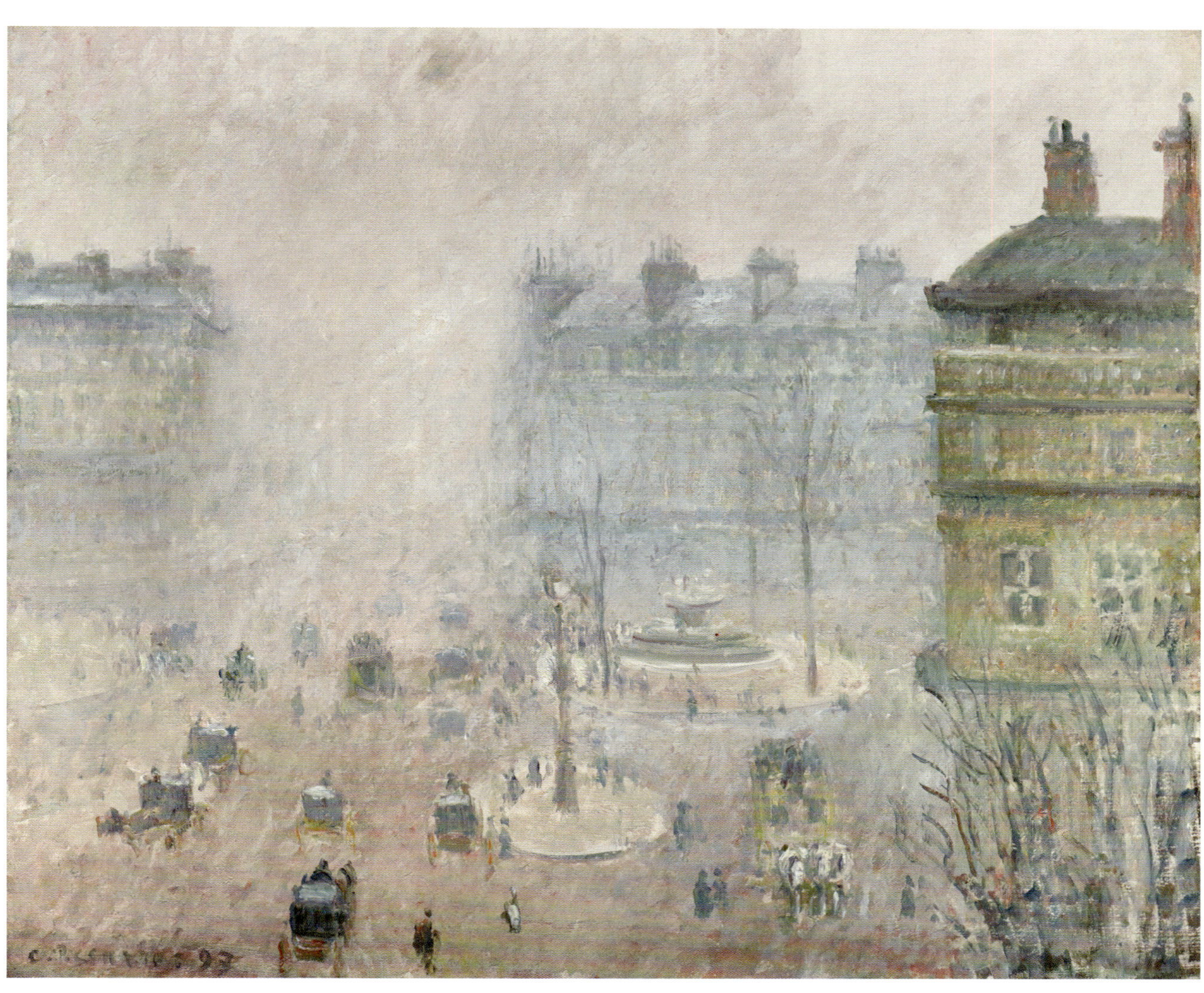

CAT. 2

Camille Pissarro
(born in Charlotte Amalie, Danish West Indies (present-day U.S. Virgin Islands), 1830–
died in Paris, France, 1903)

Place du Théâtre Français: Fog Effect
1897
Oil on canvas, 21 ½ × 26 ⅛ in. (54.6 × 66.4 cm)
Dallas Museum of Art, The Wendy and Emery Reves Collection, 1985.R.50

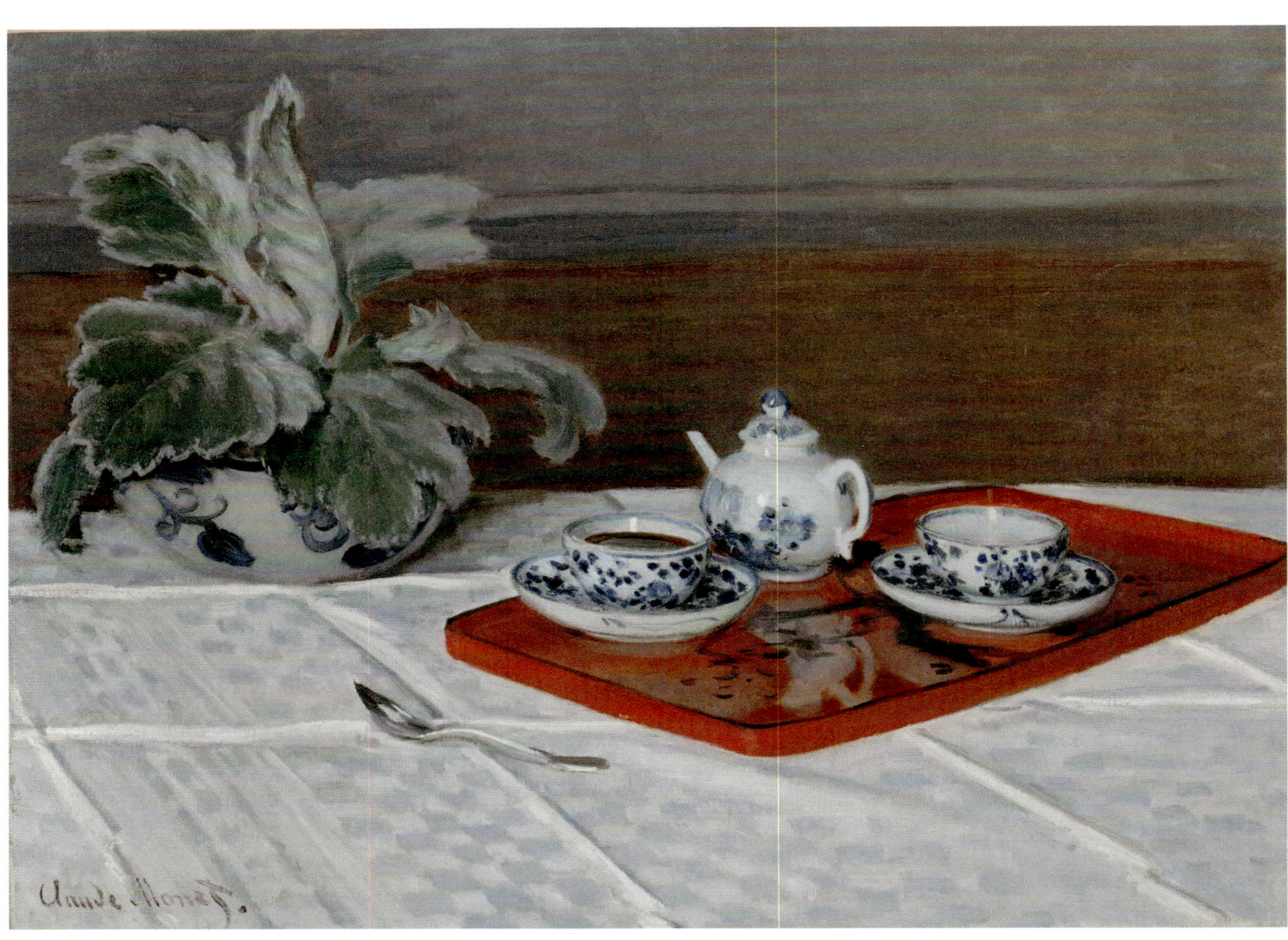

CAT. 3

Claude Monet
(born in Paris, France, 1840–died in Giverny, France, 1926)
Still Life, Tea Service
1872
Oil on canvas, 21 × 28 ⅝ in. (53.3 × 72.7 cm)
Dallas Museum of Art, The Eugene and Margaret McDermott Art Fund, Inc.,
bequest of Mrs. Eugene McDermott, 2019.67.12.McD

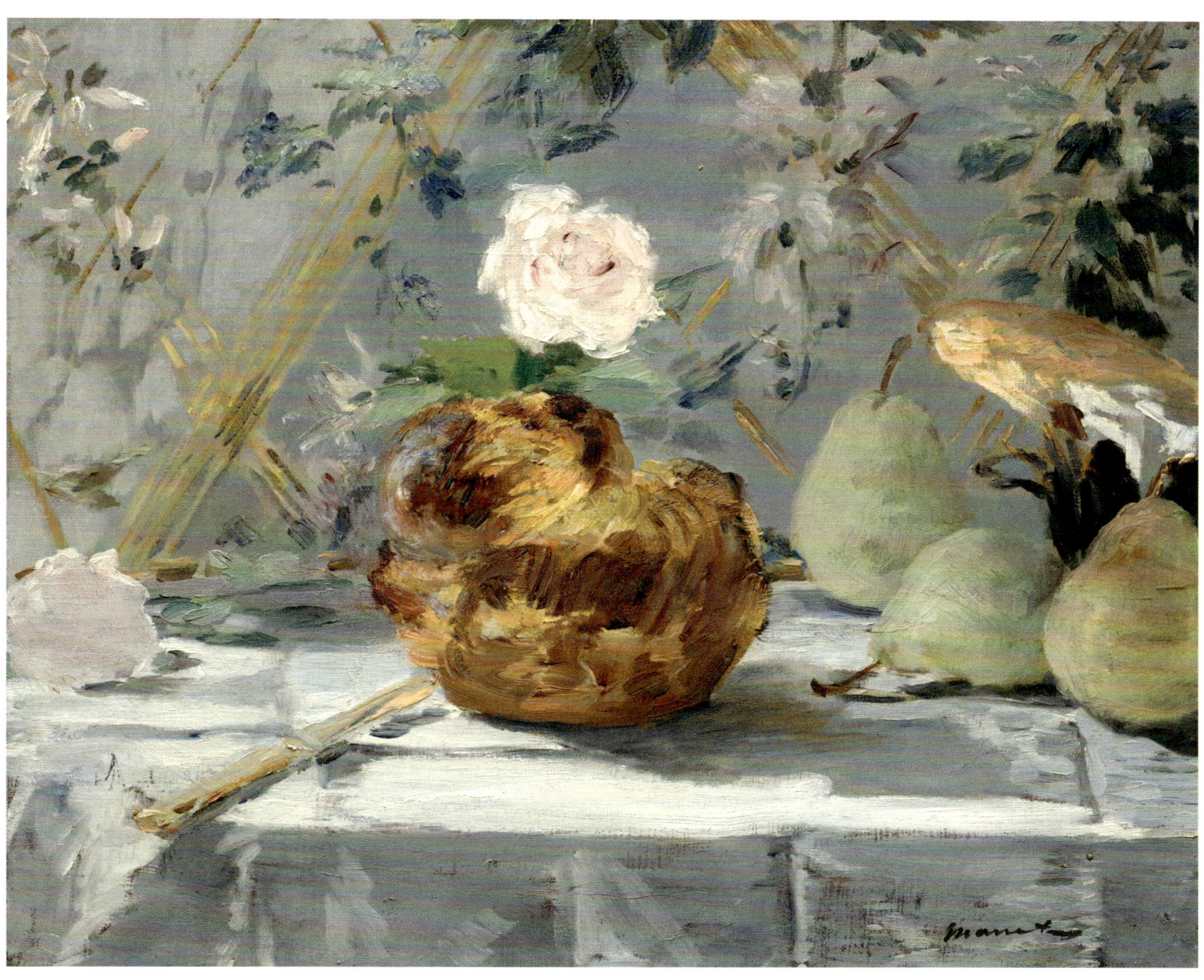

CAT. 4

Edouard Manet
(born in Paris, France, 1832–died in Paris, France, 1883)
Brioche with Pears
1876
Oil on canvas, 18 ⅛ x 22 in. (46.0 × 57.8 cm)
Dallas Museum of Art, gift of the Wendy and Emery
Reves Foundation, 2024.R.2

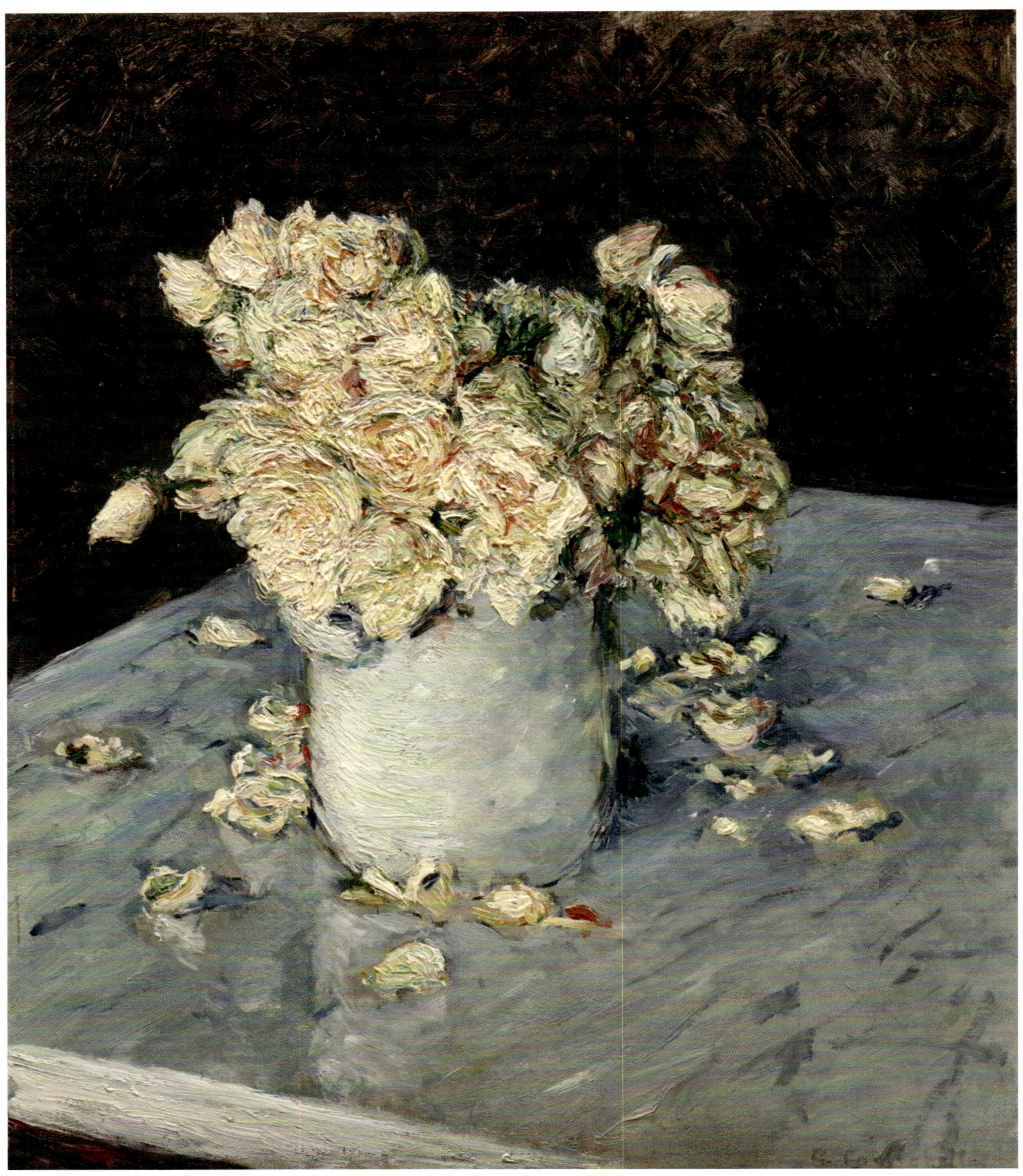

CAT. 5

Gustave Caillebotte
(born in Paris, France, 1848–died in Gennevilliers, France, 1894)

Yellow Roses in a Vase
1882
Oil on canvas, 21 × 18 ¼ in. (53.3 × 46.4 cm)
Dallas Museum of Art, The Eugene and Margaret McDermott Art Fund, Inc.,
in honor of Janet Kendall Forsythe, 2010.13.McD

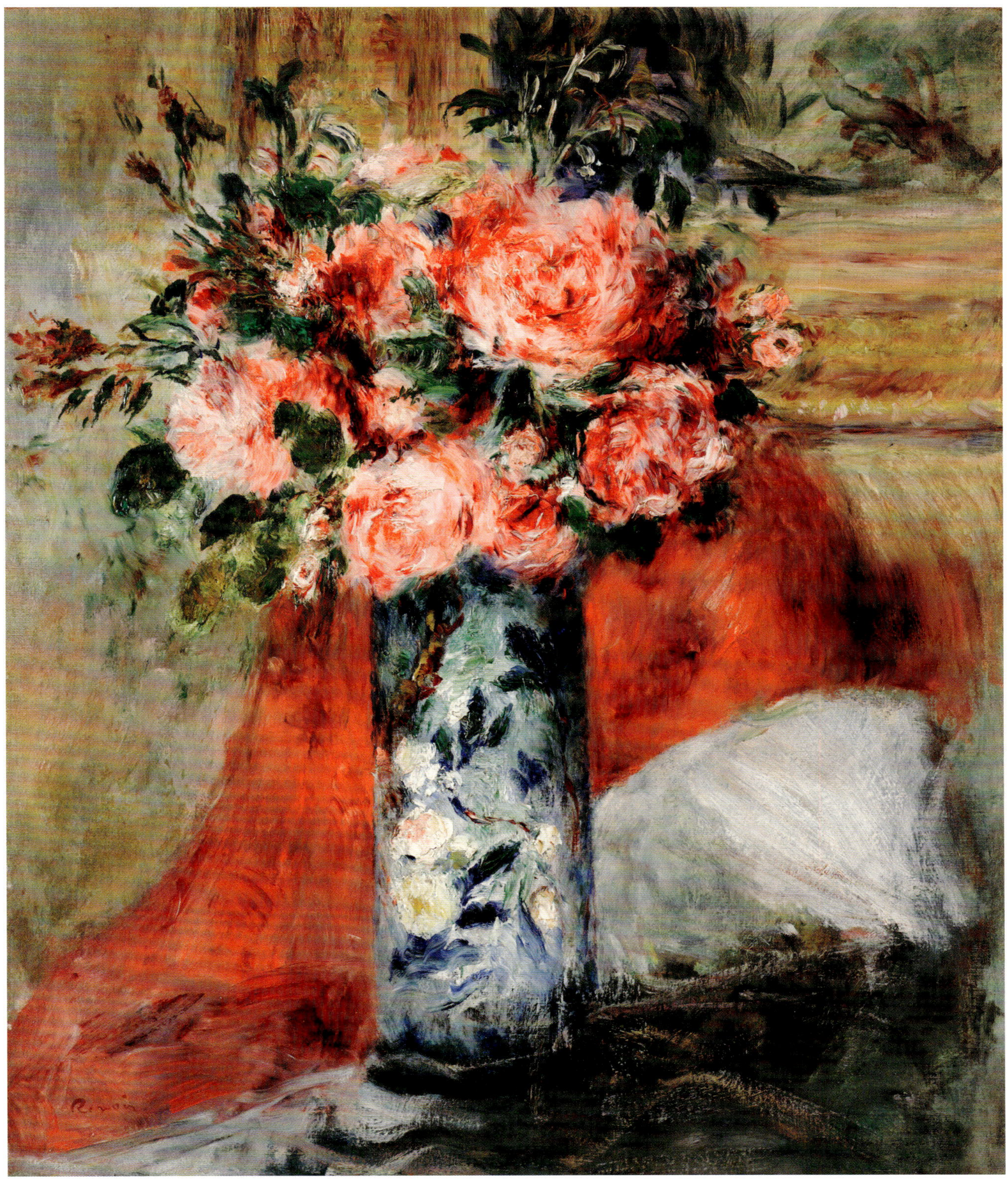

CAT. 6

Pierre-Auguste Renoir
(born in Limoges, France, 1841–died in Cagnes-sur-Mer, France, 1919)
Roses and Peonies in a Vase
1876
Oil on canvas, 23 ⅞ × 20 ¼ in. (60.6 × 51.4 cm)
Dallas Museum of Art, The Eugene and Margaret McDermott Art Fund, Inc.,
bequest of Mrs. Eugene McDermott in honor of Sarah Perot, 2019.67.22.McD

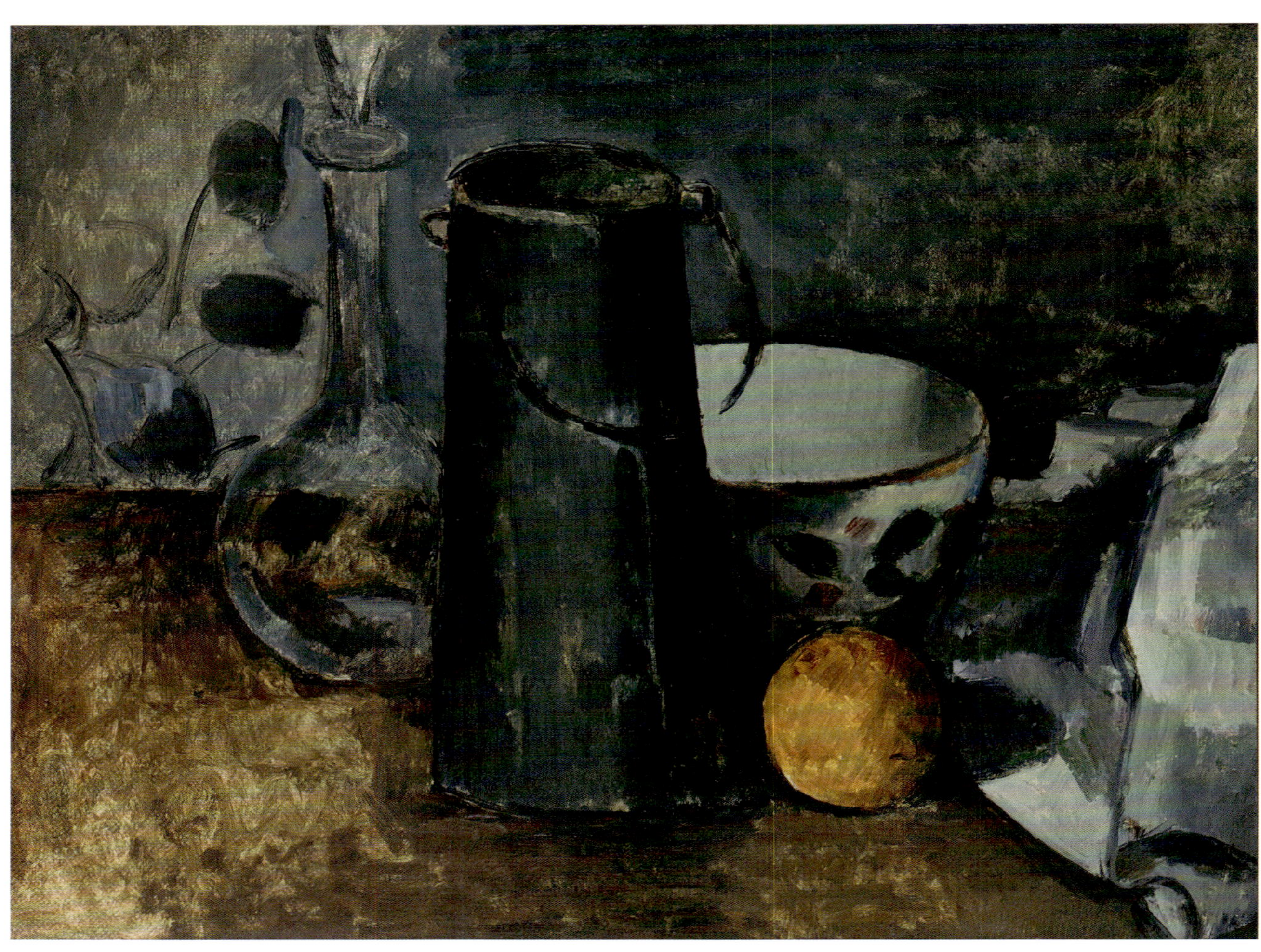

CAT. 7

Paul Cézanne
(born in Aix-en-Provence, France, 1839–died in Aix-en-Provence, France, 1906)
Still Life with Carafe, Milk Can, Bowl, and Orange
1879–1880
Oil on canvas, 10 ⅝ × 13 ¾ in. (27.0 × 34.9 cm)
Dallas Museum of Art, The Wendy and Emery Reves Collection, 1985.R.10

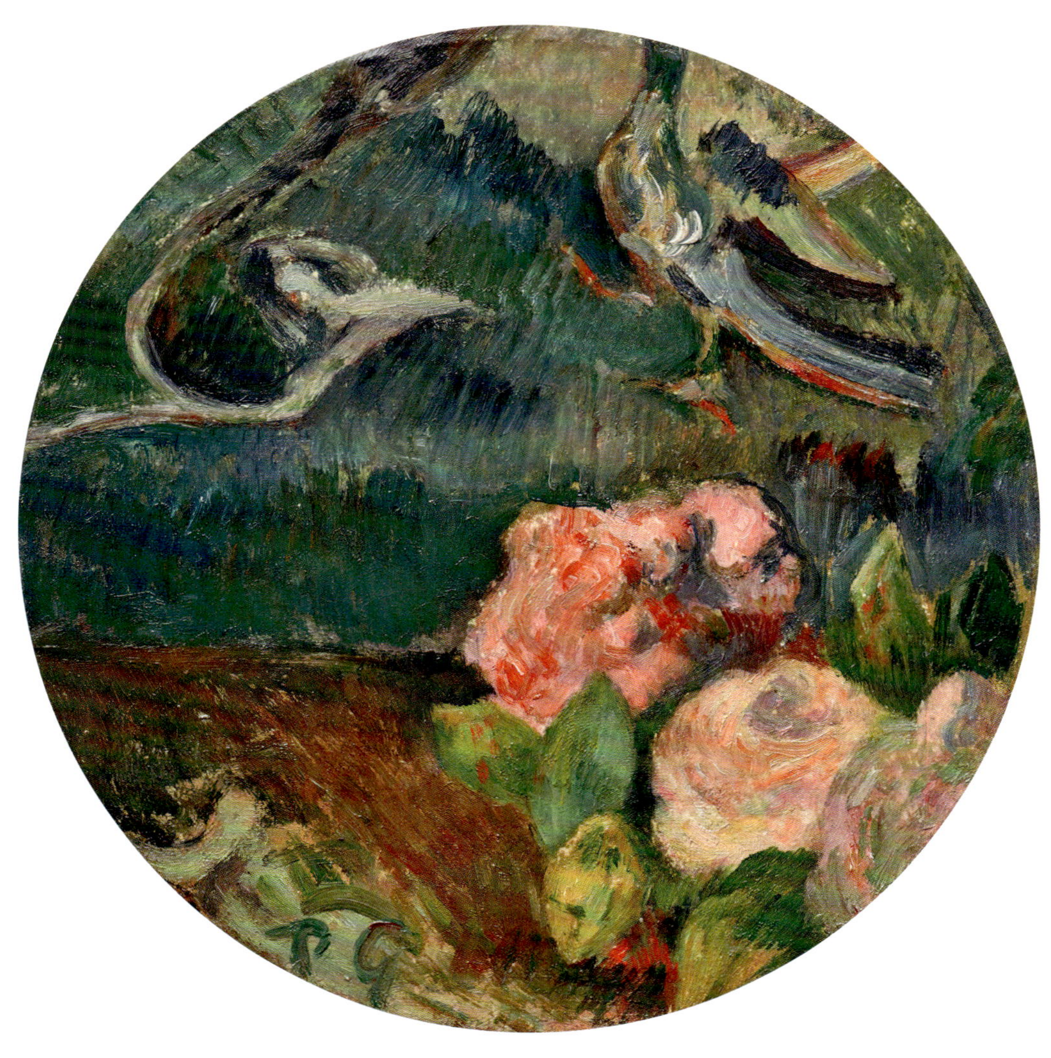

CAT. 8

Paul Gauguin
(born in Paris, France, 1848–died in Atuona, Hiva Oa, French Polynesia, 1903)

Flowers and Bird
c. 1884–1886
Drum with oil on vellum, 8 ½ × 8 × 1 ⅜ in. (21.6 × 20.3 × 3.5 cm)
Dallas Museum of Art, Irene H. and Earnest G. Wadel Acquisition Fund, 2019.26

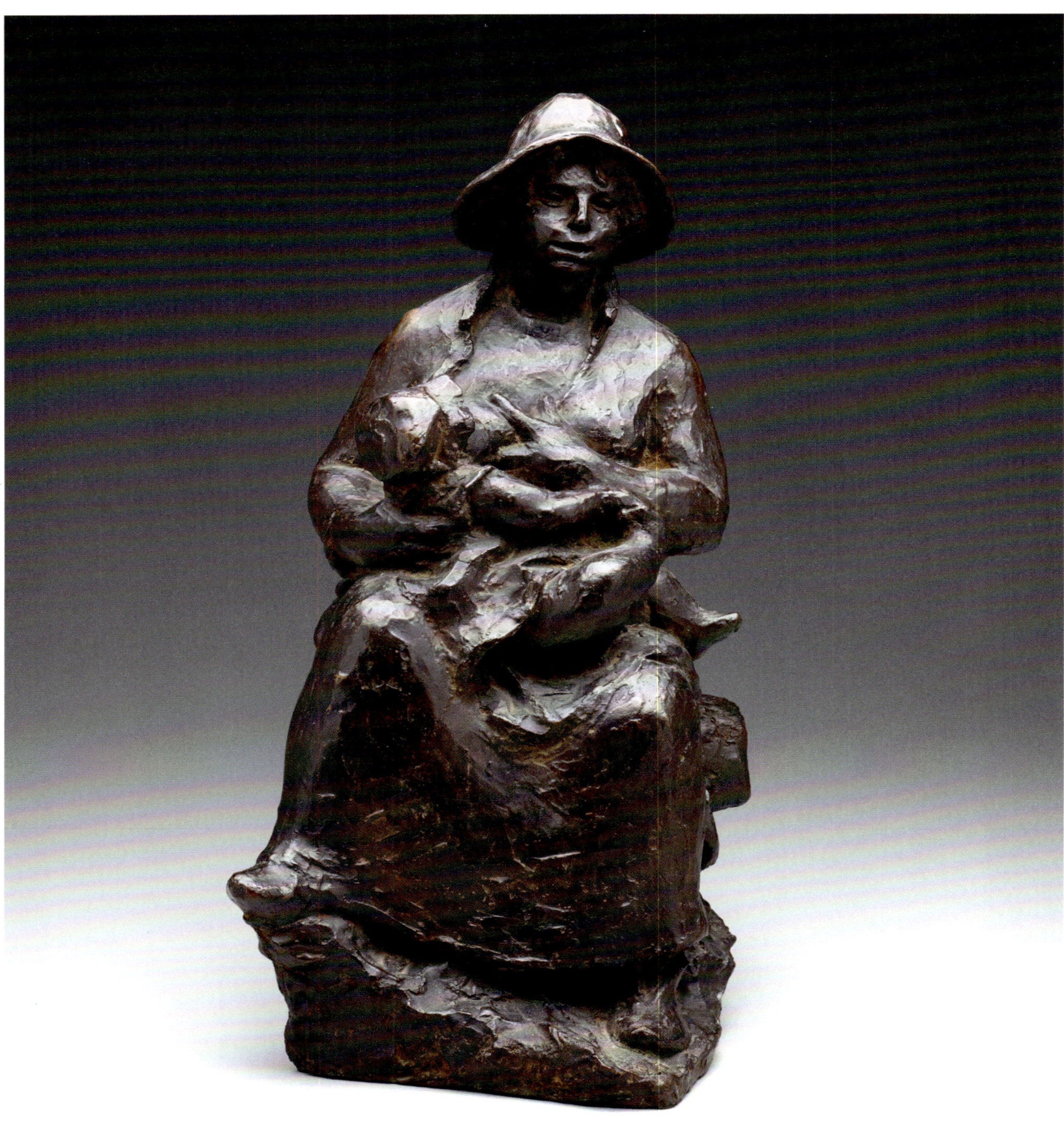

CAT. 9

Pierre-Auguste Renoir
(born in Limoges, France, 1841–died in Cagnes-sur-Mer, France, 1919)
Richard Guino
(born in Girona, Spain, 1890–died in Antony, France, 1973)
Mother and Child
Modeled 1915; cast posthumously 1928
Bronze, 21 ¼ × 10 × 12 ¾ in. (54.0 × 25.4 × 32.4 cm)
Dallas Museum of Art, gift of Cornelia and Ralph Heins in honor of
Elinor Heins, 2021.32.18

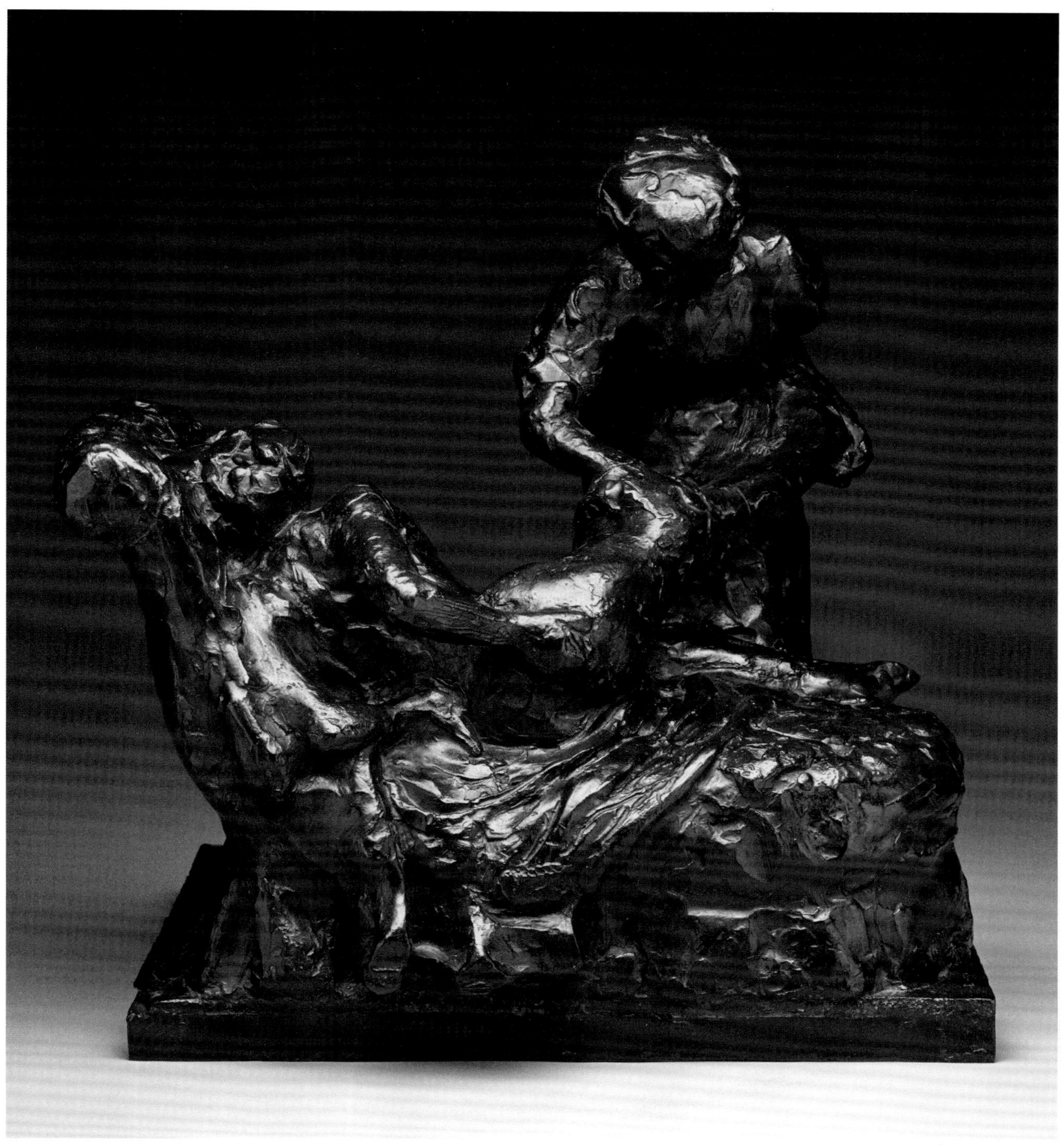

CAT. 10

Edgar Degas
(born in Paris, France, 1834–died in Paris, France, 1917)
The Masseuse
Modeled between 1896 and 1911; cast after 1917
Bronze, 17 × 15 × 12 ½ in. (43.2 × 38.1 × 31.8 cm)
Dallas Museum of Art, The Eugene and Margaret McDermott
Art Fund, Inc., 1965.26.McD

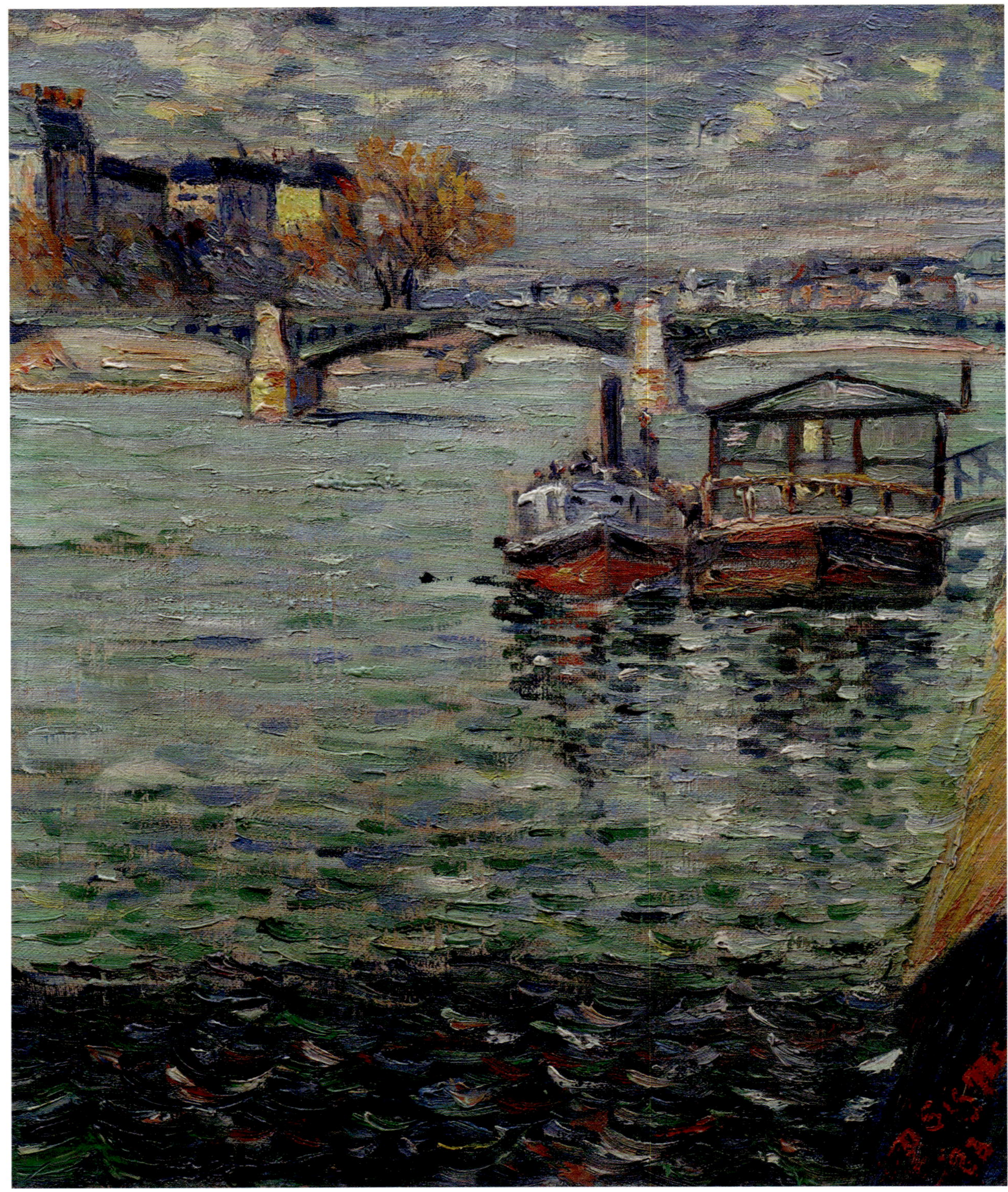

CAT. 11

Paul Signac
(born in Paris, France, 1863–died in Paris, France, 1935)
The Seine River in Paris
1883
Oil on canvas, 14 × 11 in. (35.6 × 27.9 cm)
Dallas Museum of Art, gift of Cornelia and Ralph Heins in
memory of Elinor Heins, 2023.79.3

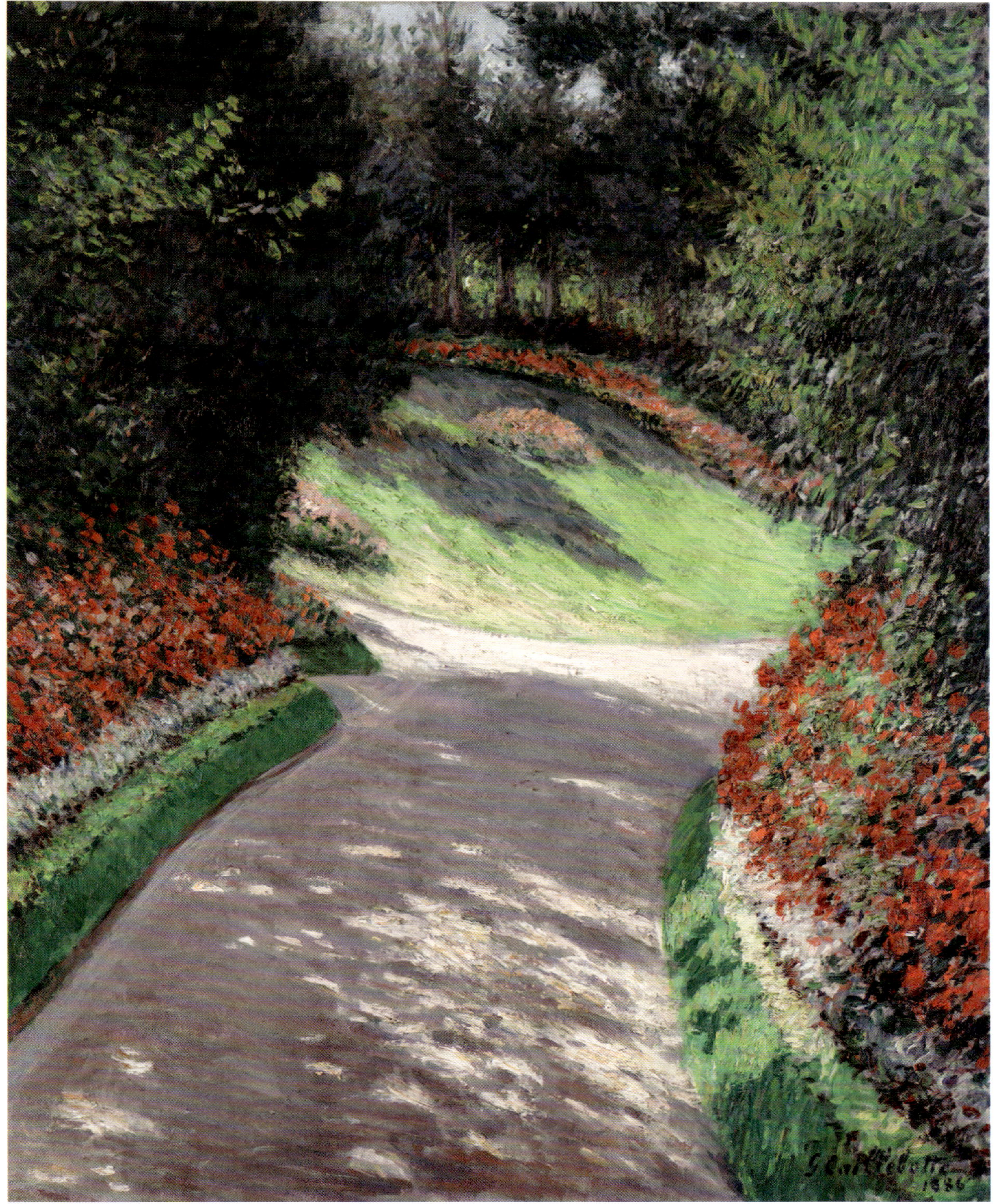

CAT. 12

Gustave Caillebotte
(born in Paris, France, 1848–died in Gennevilliers, France, 1894)
The Path in the Garden
1886
Oil on canvas, 32 ⅛ × 28 ⅞ in. (81.6 × 73.3 cm)
Dallas Museum of Art, The Eugene and Margaret McDermott Art Fund, Inc.,
bequest of Mrs. Eugene McDermott, 2019.67.5.McD

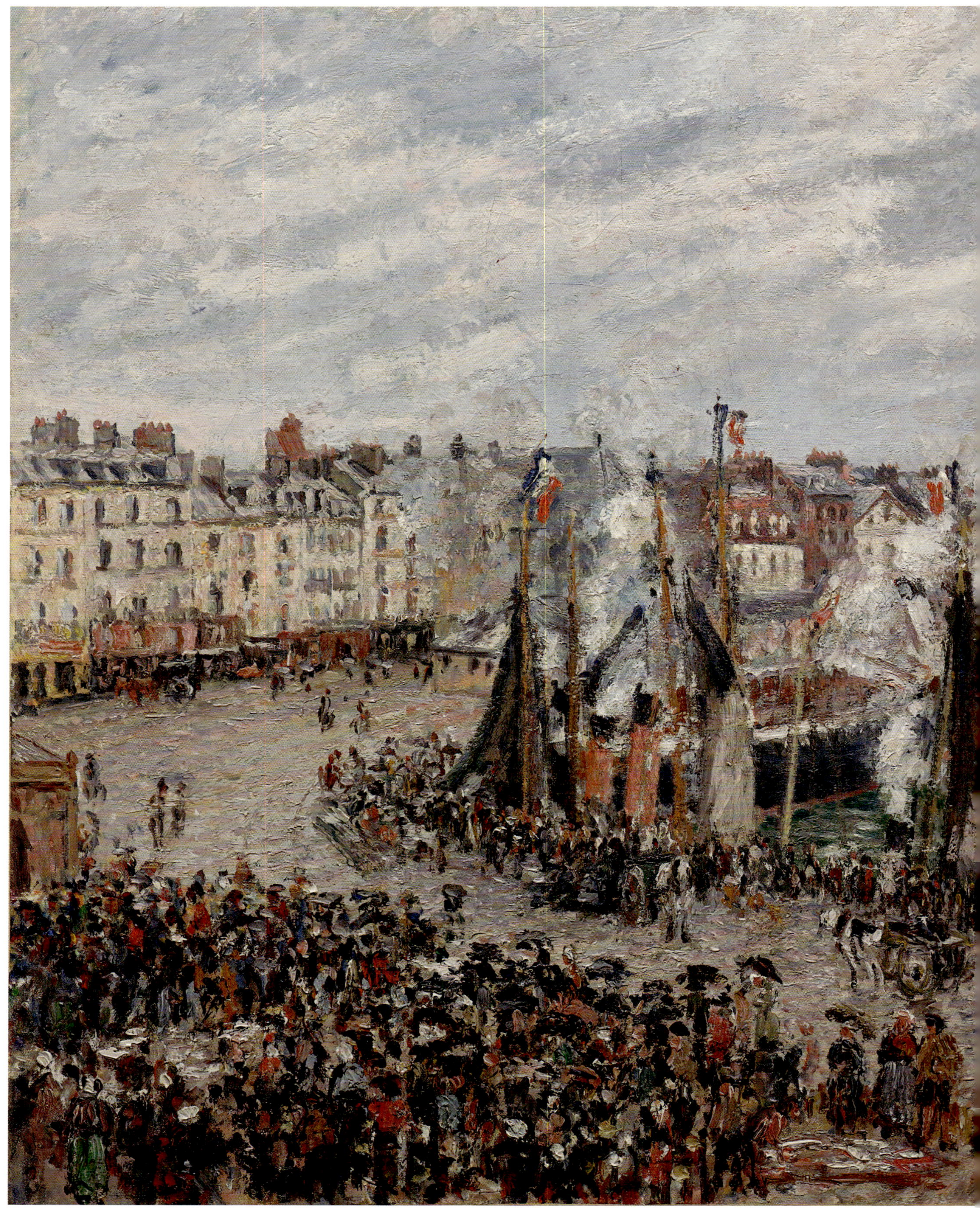

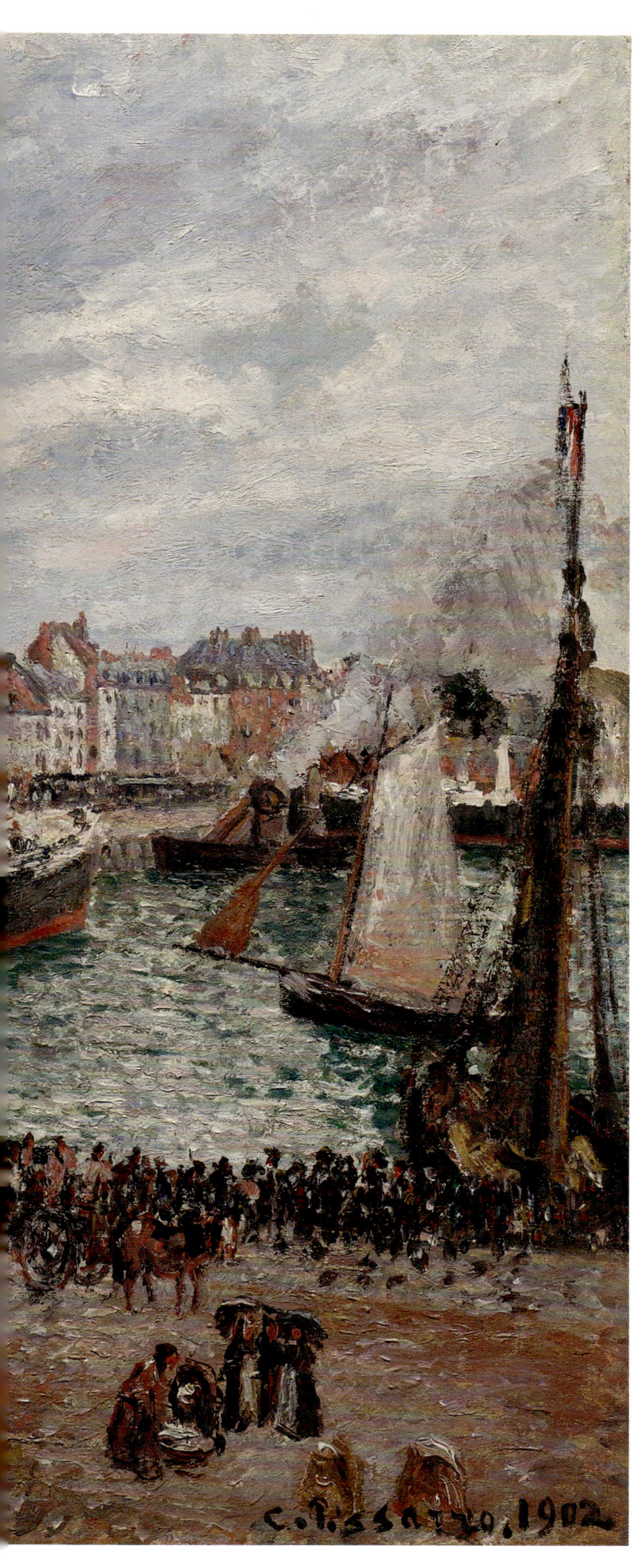

CAT. 13

Camille Pissarro
(born in Charlotte Amalie, Danish West Indies (present-day U.S. Virgin Islands),
1830–died in Paris, France, 1903)
The Fish Market, Dieppe: Grey Weather, Morning
1902
Oil on canvas, 25 ¾ × 31 ⅞ in. (65.4 × 81.0 cm)
Dallas Museum of Art, The Eugene and Margaret McDermott Art Fund, Inc.,
bequest of Mrs. Eugene McDermott, 2019.67.20.McD

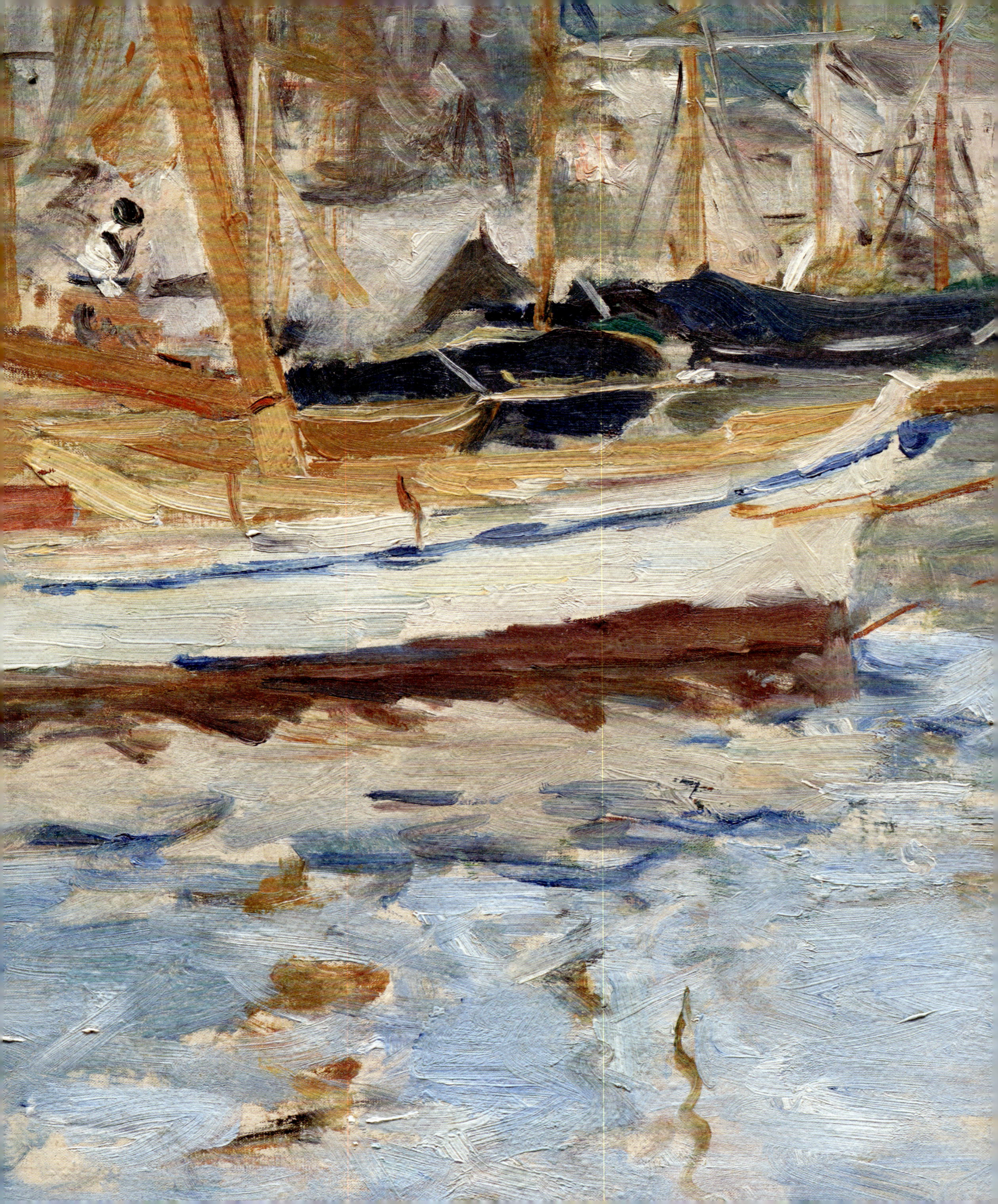

Field Notes

THE IMPRESSIONISTS' radical approach extended beyond their subjects to their techniques and materials. Fueled by technological advances, such as the invention of the resealable metal paint tube and the expansion of France's railways, nearly all of the Impressionists took their canvases outdoors to transcribe the sensation of light and movement, whether in and around France's capital or further afield to its coasts and southern regions.

To capture such fleeting effects, they rapidly applied bright pigments on reflective grounds in broken, textured brushstrokes. They experimented with cutting-edge color theories, such as painting contrasting complementaries side by side to boost each color's vibrancy, and avoided black and gray in their depiction of shadows and volume. They also chose not to apply shiny varnish, the final step in Academic painting that signified a finished picture.

The Impressionists' vivid colors and dissolving forms stunned contemporary viewers, who were accustomed to the slick realism and earth-toned palettes of Academic paintings shown at the Paris Salon. Most critics and collectors saw Impressionist paintings as clumsy and sketch-like at best, and garishly ugly at worst.

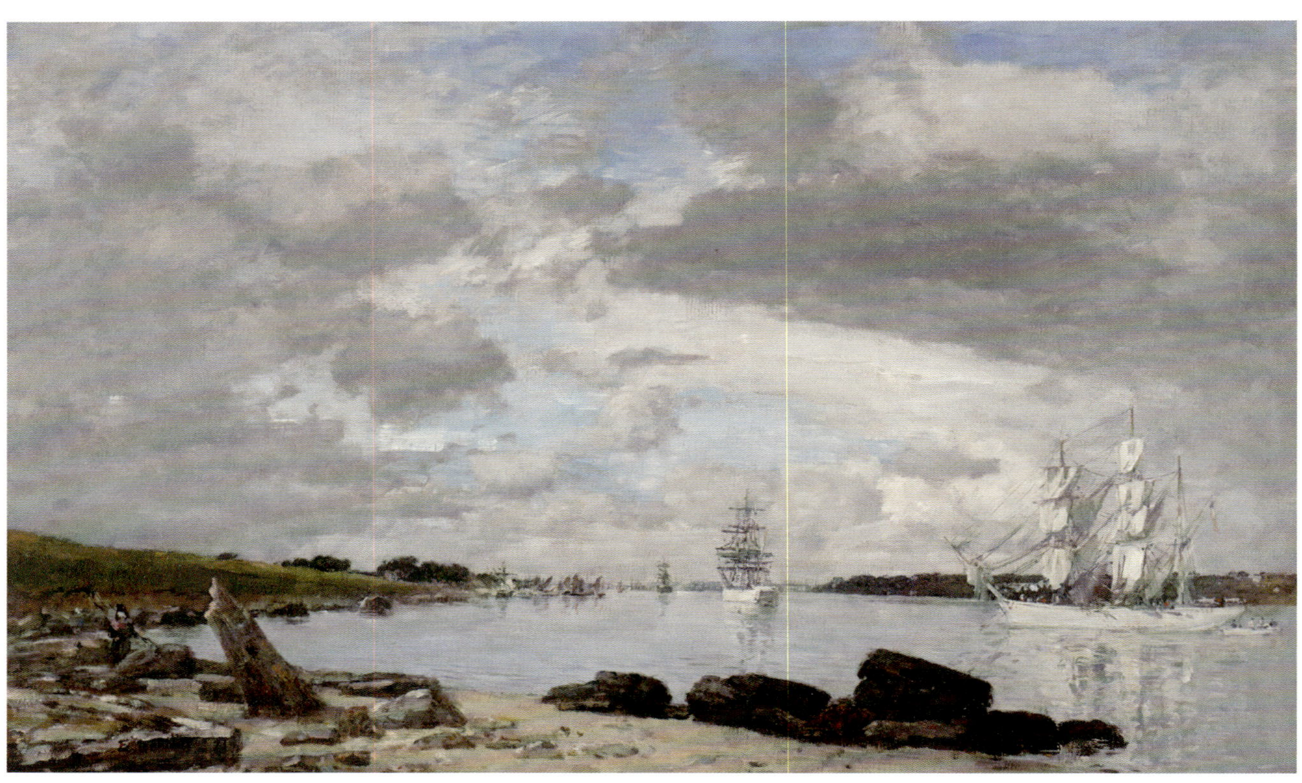

CAT. 14

Eugène-Louis Boudin
(born in Honfleur, France, 1824–died in Deauville, France, 1898)
The Bay at the Mouth of the River Elorn, Landerneau
1871
Oil on canvas, 15 ⅞ × 25 ¾ in. (40.3 × 65.4 cm)
Dallas Museum of Art, The Eugene and Margaret McDermott Art Fund, Inc.,
bequest of Mrs. Eugene McDermott, 2019.67.2.McD

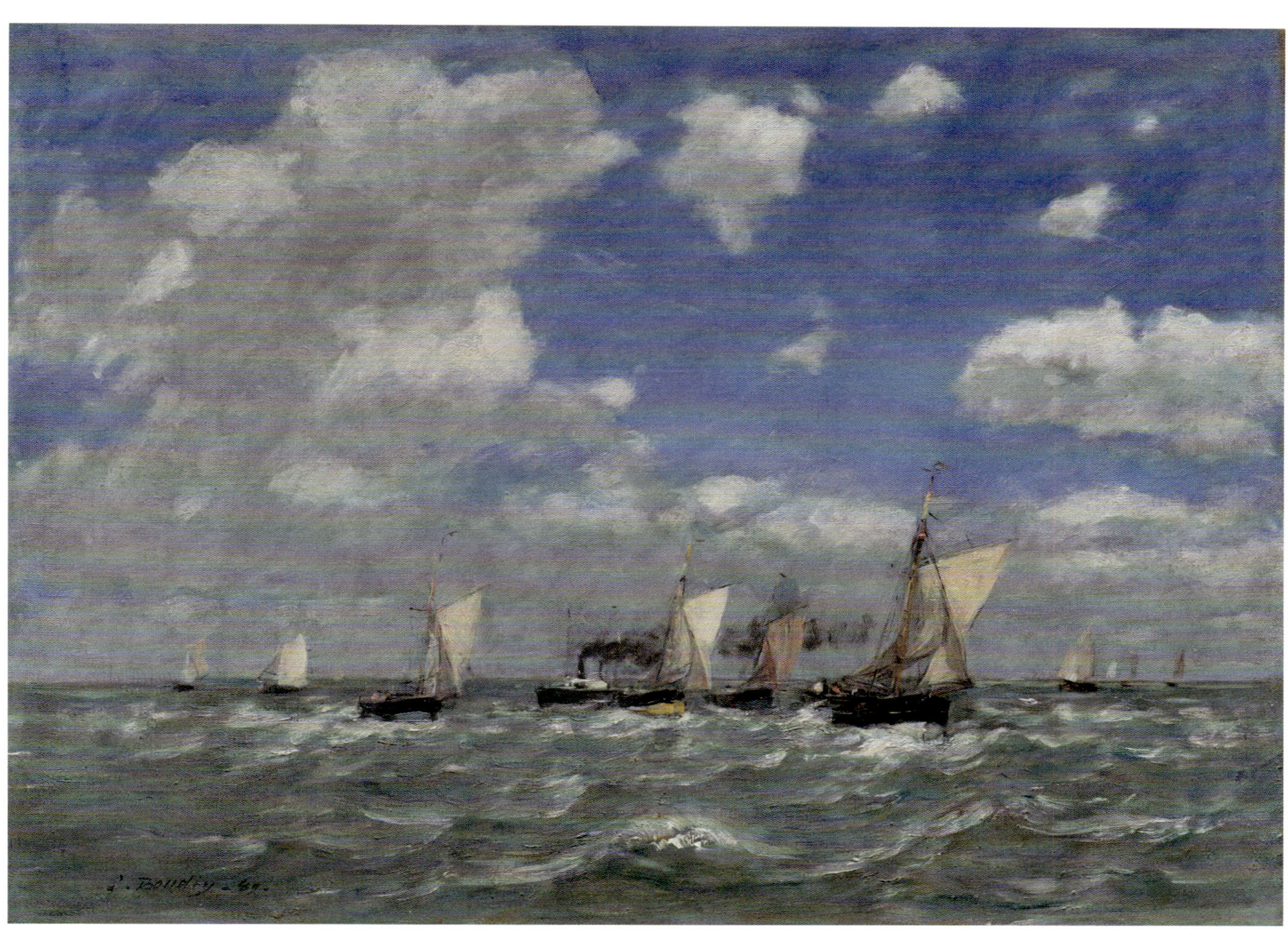

CAT. 15

Eugène-Louis Boudin
(born in Honfleur, France, 1824–died in Deauville, France, 1898)

Open Sea
1889
Oil on canvas, 16 ¼ × 21 ⅞ in. (41.3 × 55.6 cm)
Dallas Museum of Art, gift of Cornelia and Ralph Heins in memory
of Elinor Heins, 2021.32.5

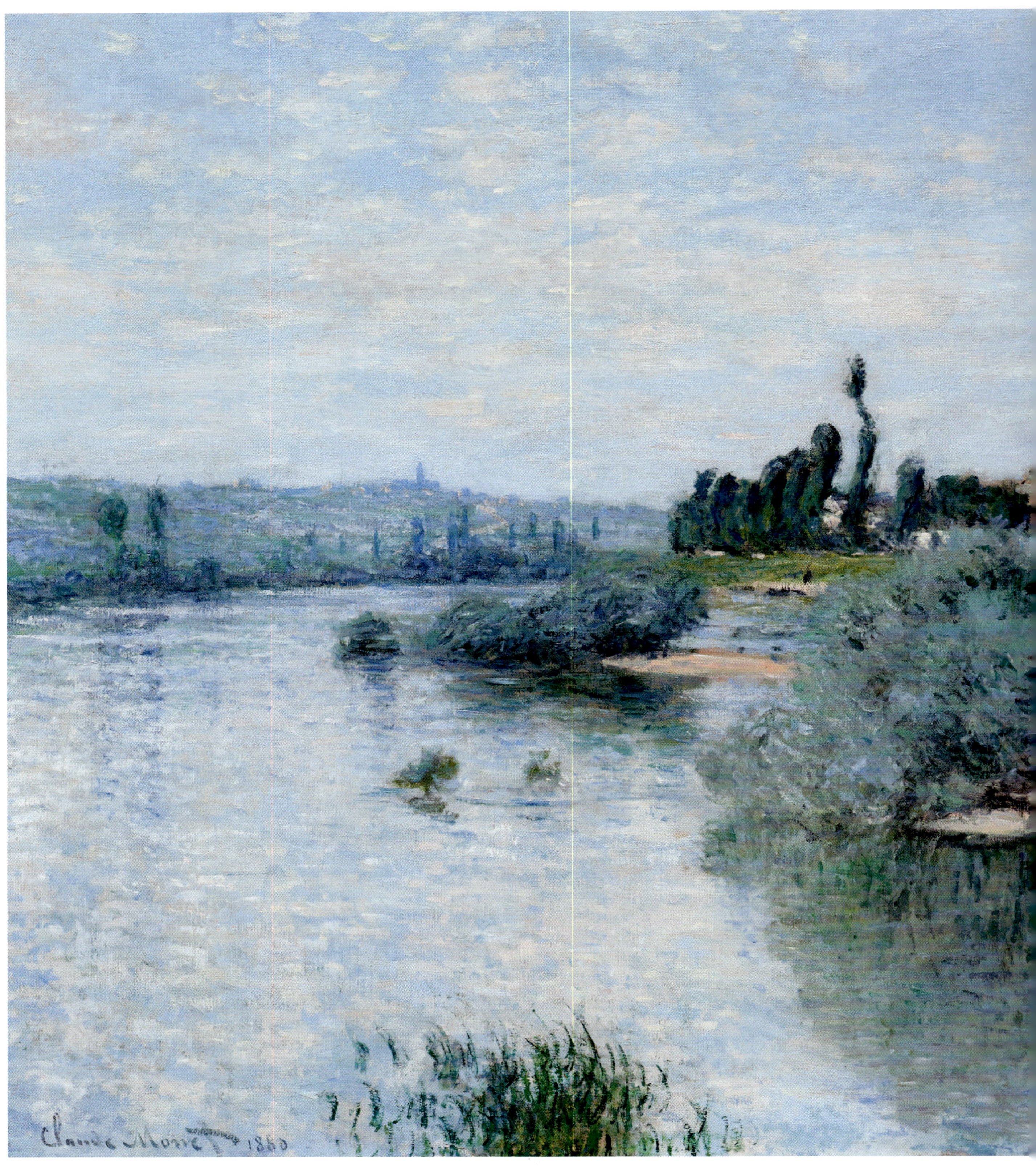
Claude Monet 1880

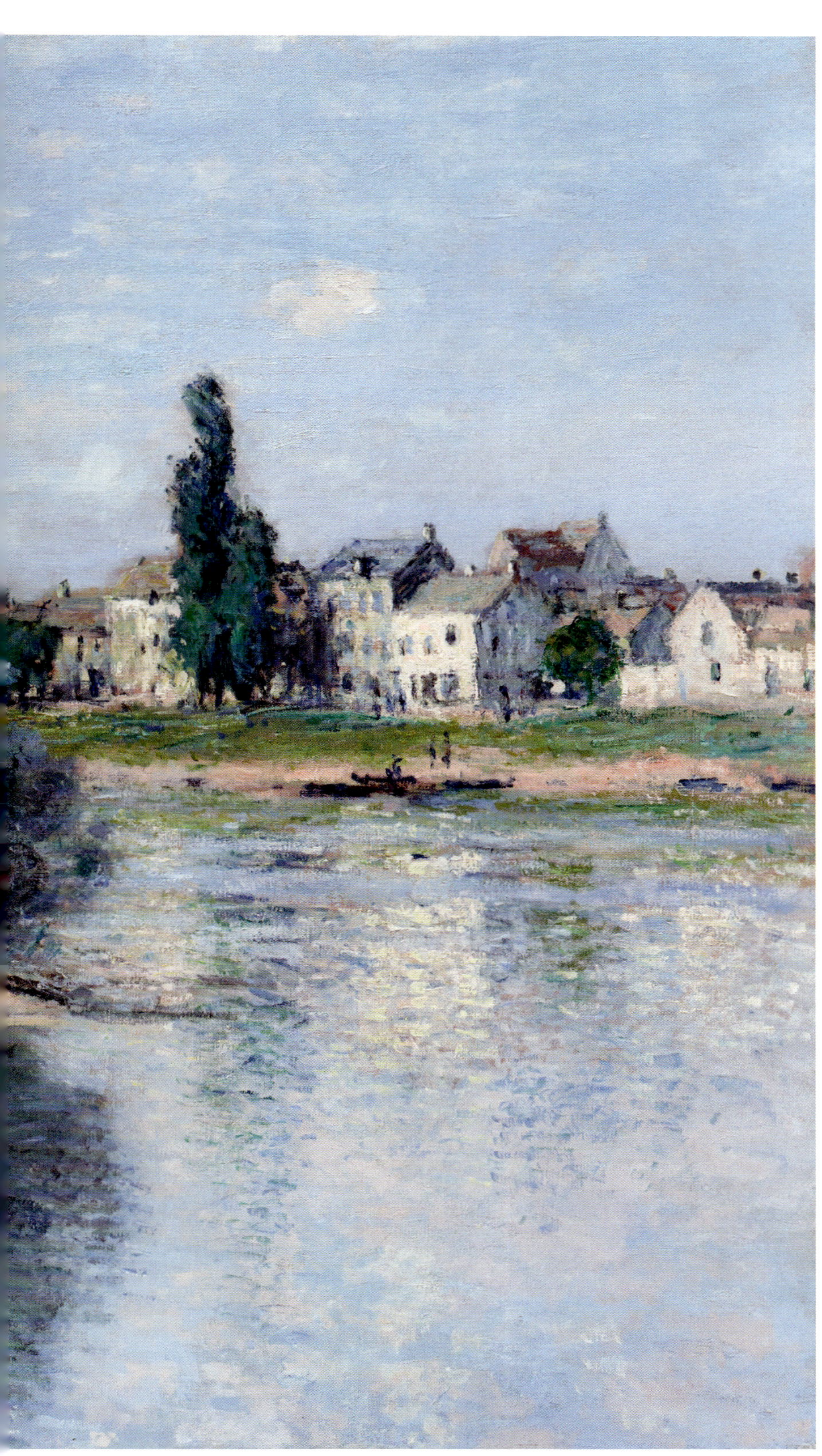

CAT. 16

Claude Monet
(born in Paris, France, 1840–died in Giverny, France, 1926)
The Seine at Lavacourt
1880
Oil on canvas, 38 ¾ x 58 ¾ in. (98.4 x 149.2 cm)
Dallas Museum of Art, Munger Fund, 1938.4.M

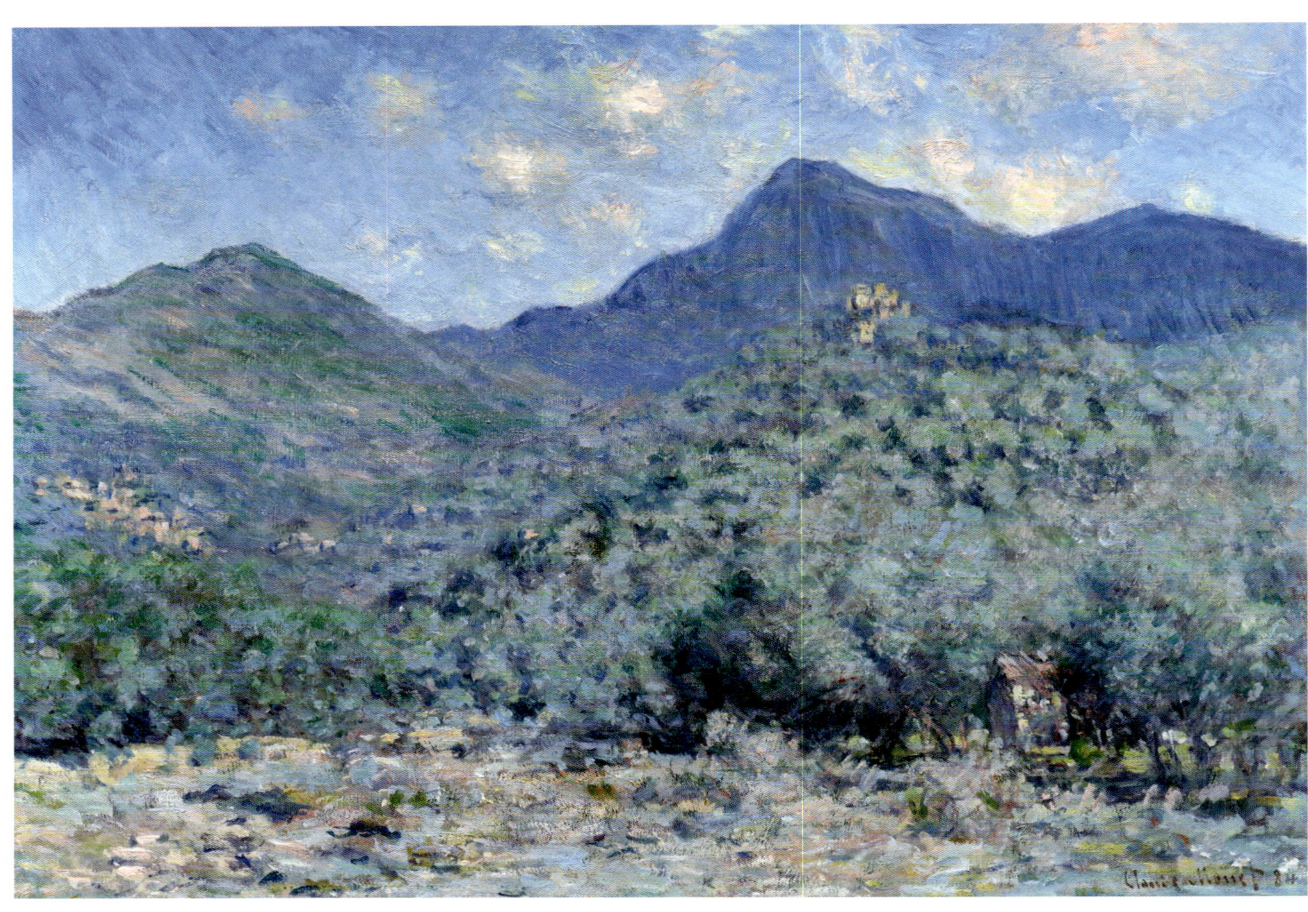

CAT. 17

Claude Monet
(born in Paris, France, 1840–died in Giverny, France, 1926)

Valle Buona, Near Bordighera
1884
Oil on canvas, 25 ⅜ × 36 in. (64.5 × 91.4 cm)
Dallas Museum of Art, gift of the Meadows Foundation, Incorporated, 1981.127

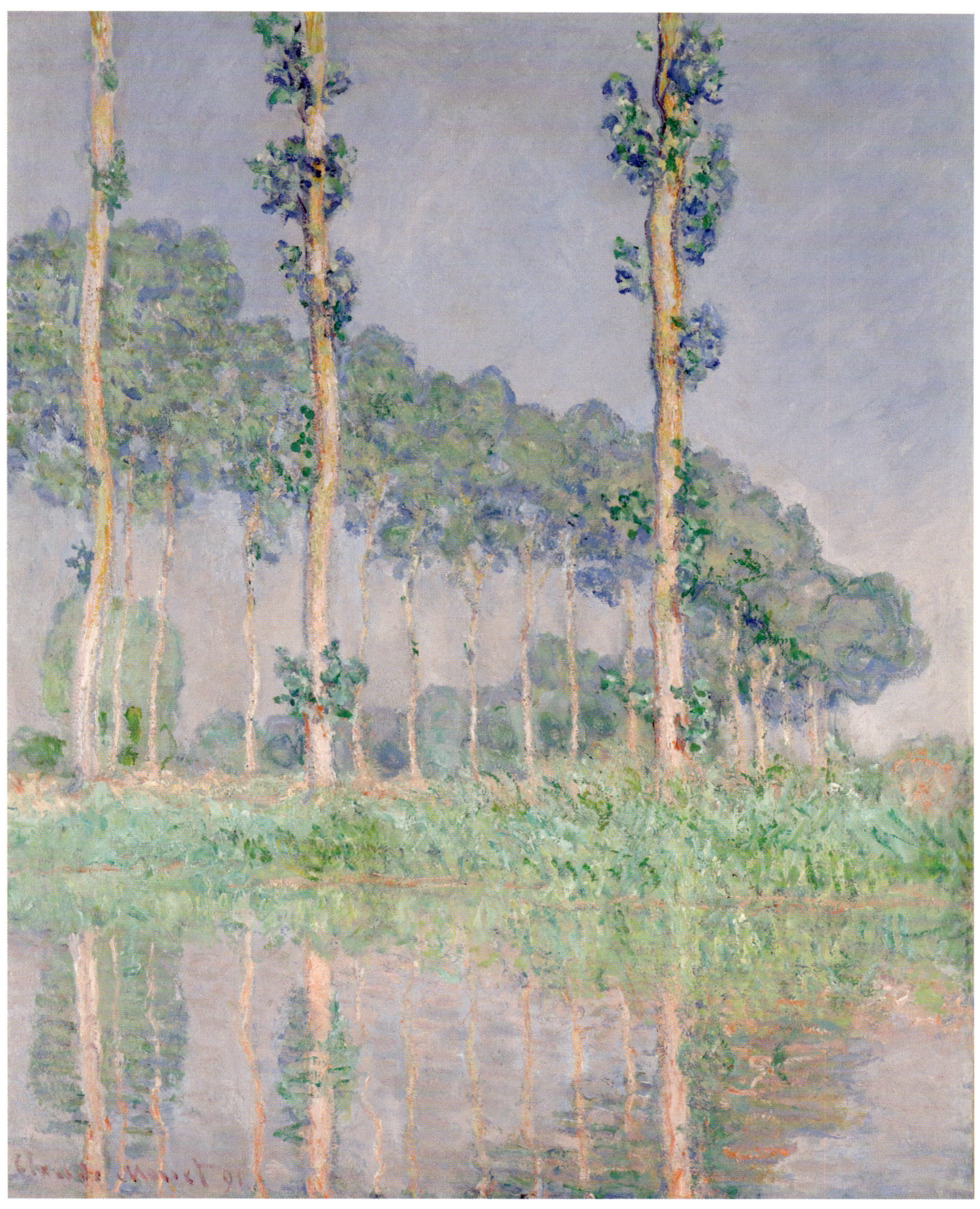

CAT. 18

Claude Monet
(born in Paris, France, 1840–died in Giverny, France, 1926)
Poplars, Pink Effect
1891
Oil on canvas, 37 × 29 ½ in. (94.0 × 74.9 cm)
Dallas Museum of Art, The Eugene and Margaret McDermott Art
Fund, Inc., bequest of Mrs. Eugene McDermott, 2019.67.14.McD

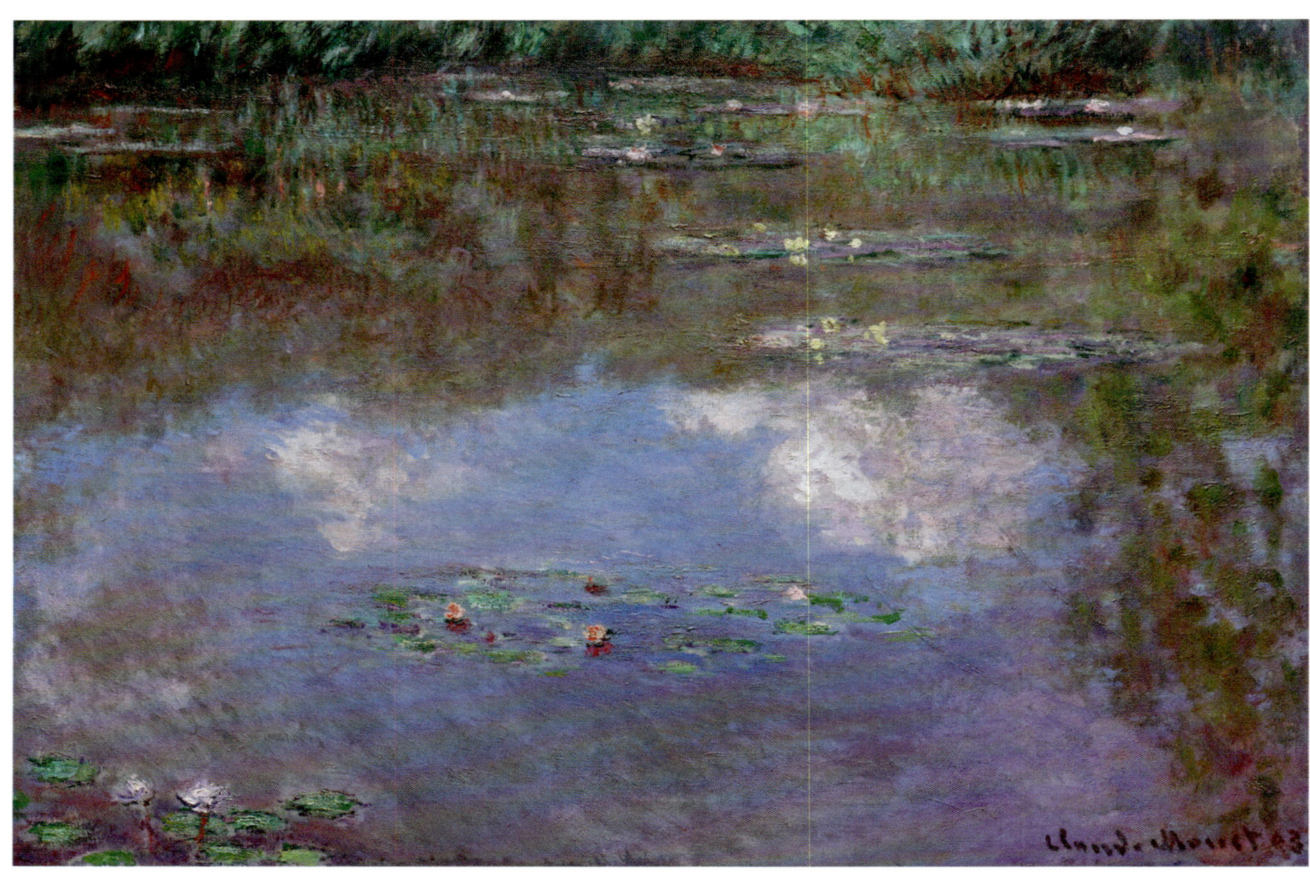

CAT. 19

Claude Monet
(born in Paris, France, 1840–died in Giverny, France, 1926)

The Water Lily Pond (Clouds)
1903
Oil on canvas, 29 ⅜ × 42 ½ in. (74.6 × 108.0 cm)
Dallas Museum of Art, The Eugene and Margaret McDermott Art Fund, Inc., bequest
of Mrs. Eugene McDermott in honor of Nancy Hamon, 2019.67.13.McD

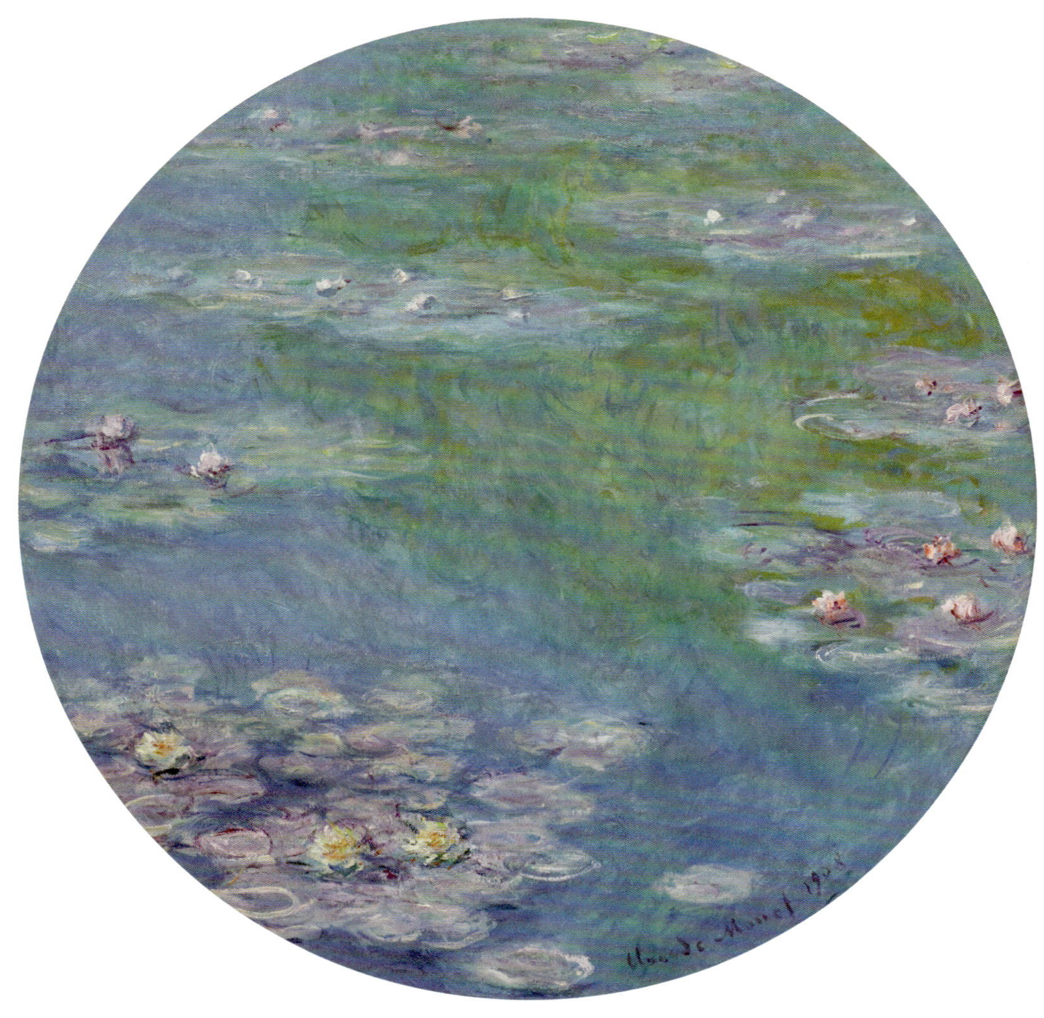

CAT. 20

Claude Monet
(born in Paris, France, 1840–died in Giverny, France, 1926)

Water Lilies
1908
Oil on canvas, 31 ½ × 31 ½ in. (80.0 x 80.0 cm)
Dallas Museum of Art, gift of the Meadows Foundation, Incorporated, 1981.128

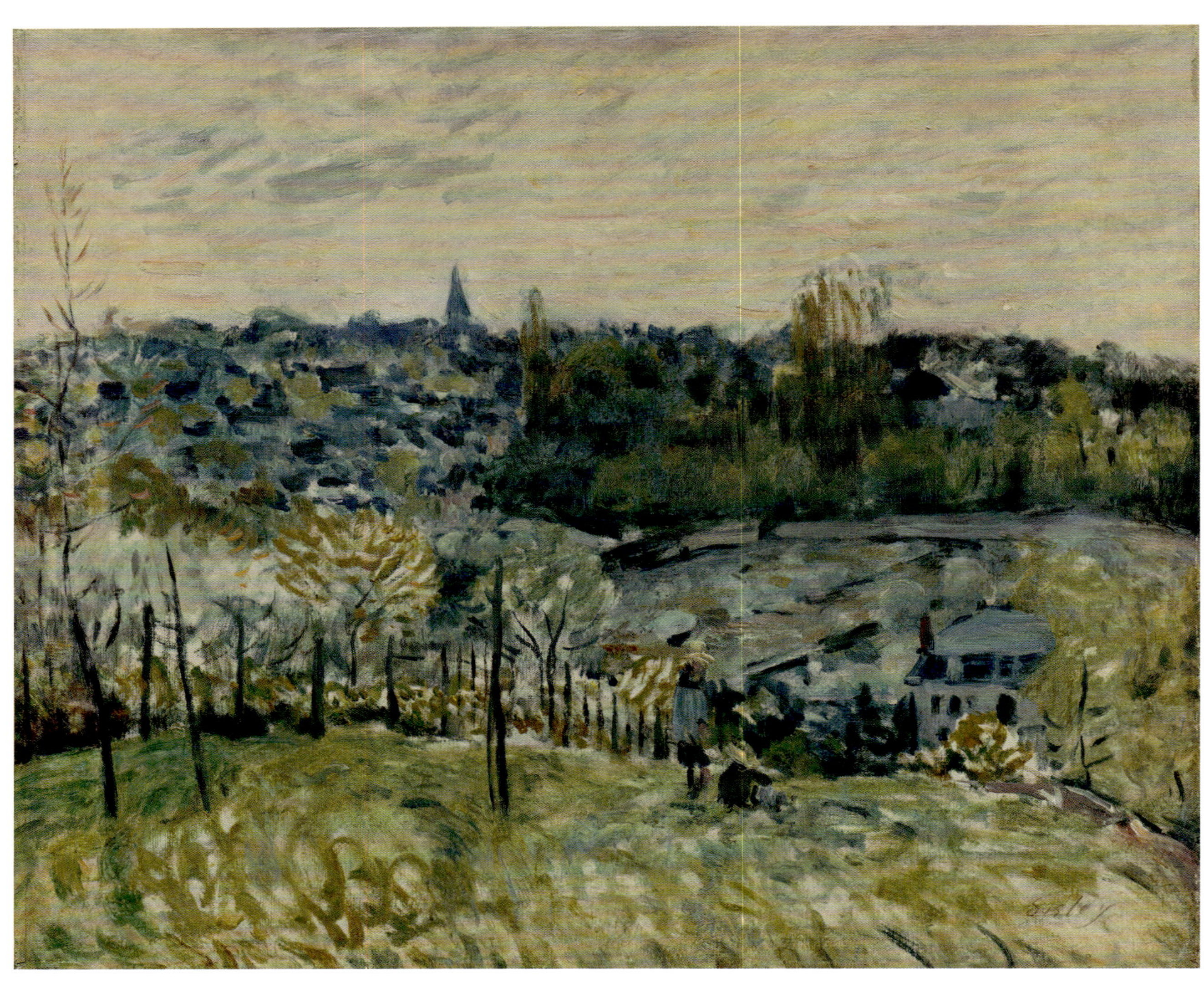

CAT. 21

Alfred Sisley
(born in Paris, France, 1839–died in Moret-sur-Loing, France, 1899)
The Village of Marly-le-Roi Seen from Louveciennes
1876
Oil on canvas, 16 ⅞ × 20 ⅜ in. (42.9 × 51.8 cm)
Dallas Museum of Art, gift of Cornelia and Ralph Heins in memory
of Elinor Heins, 2023.79.4

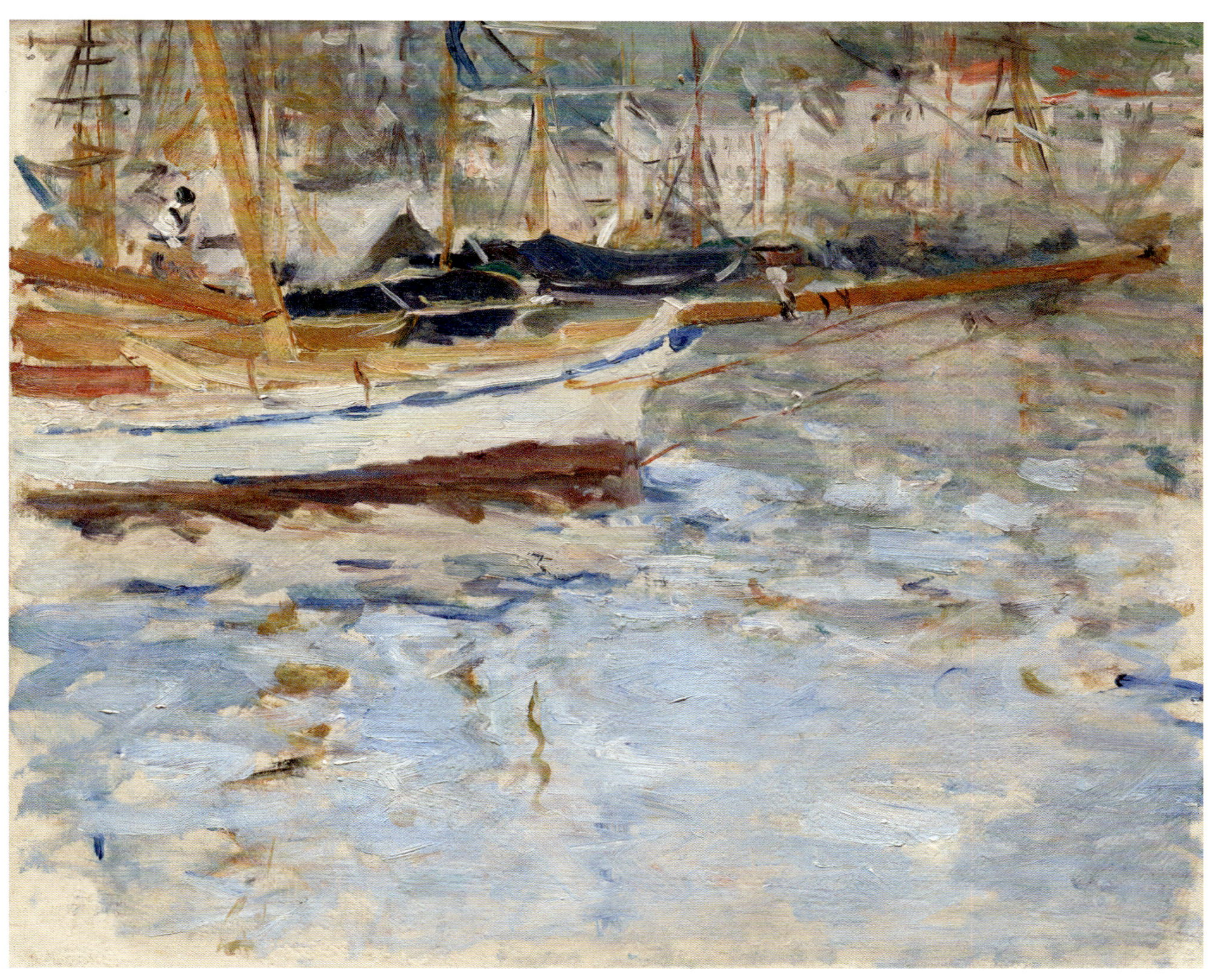

CAT. 22

Berthe Morisot
(born in Bourges, France, 1841–died in Paris, France, 1895)
The Port of Nice
1881–1882
Oil on canvas, 15 × 18 ¼ in. (38.1 × 46.4 cm)
Dallas Museum of Art, The Wendy and Emery Reves Collection, 1985.R.40

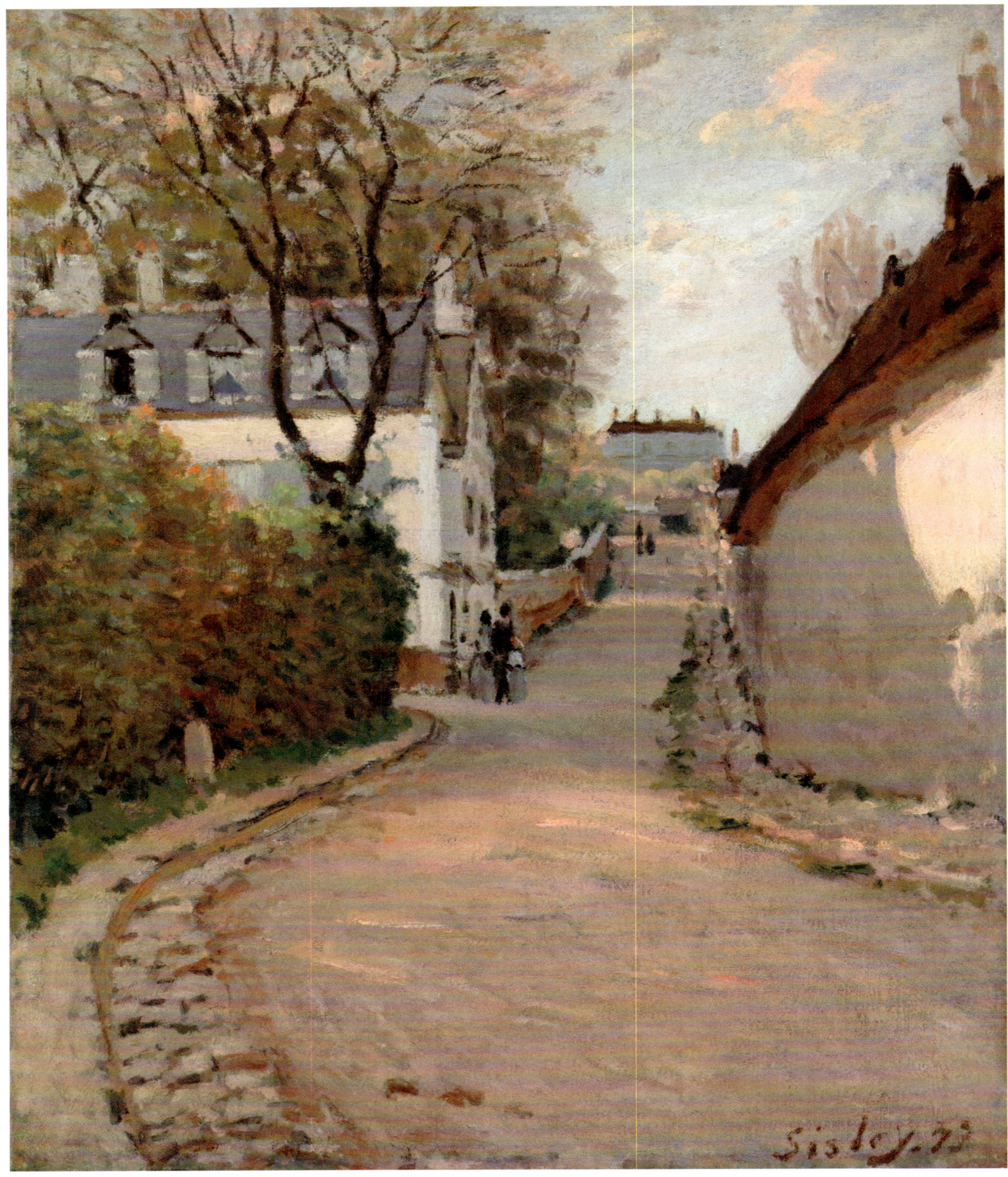

CAT. 23

Alfred Sisley
(born in Paris, France, 1839–died in Moret-sur-Loing, France, 1899)

Street in Ville-d'Avray
1873
Oil on canvas, 22 × 18 ½ in. (55.9 × 47.0 cm)
Dallas Museum of Art, The Eugene and Margaret McDermott Art Fund, Inc.,
bequest of Mrs. Eugene McDermott, 2019.67.26.McD

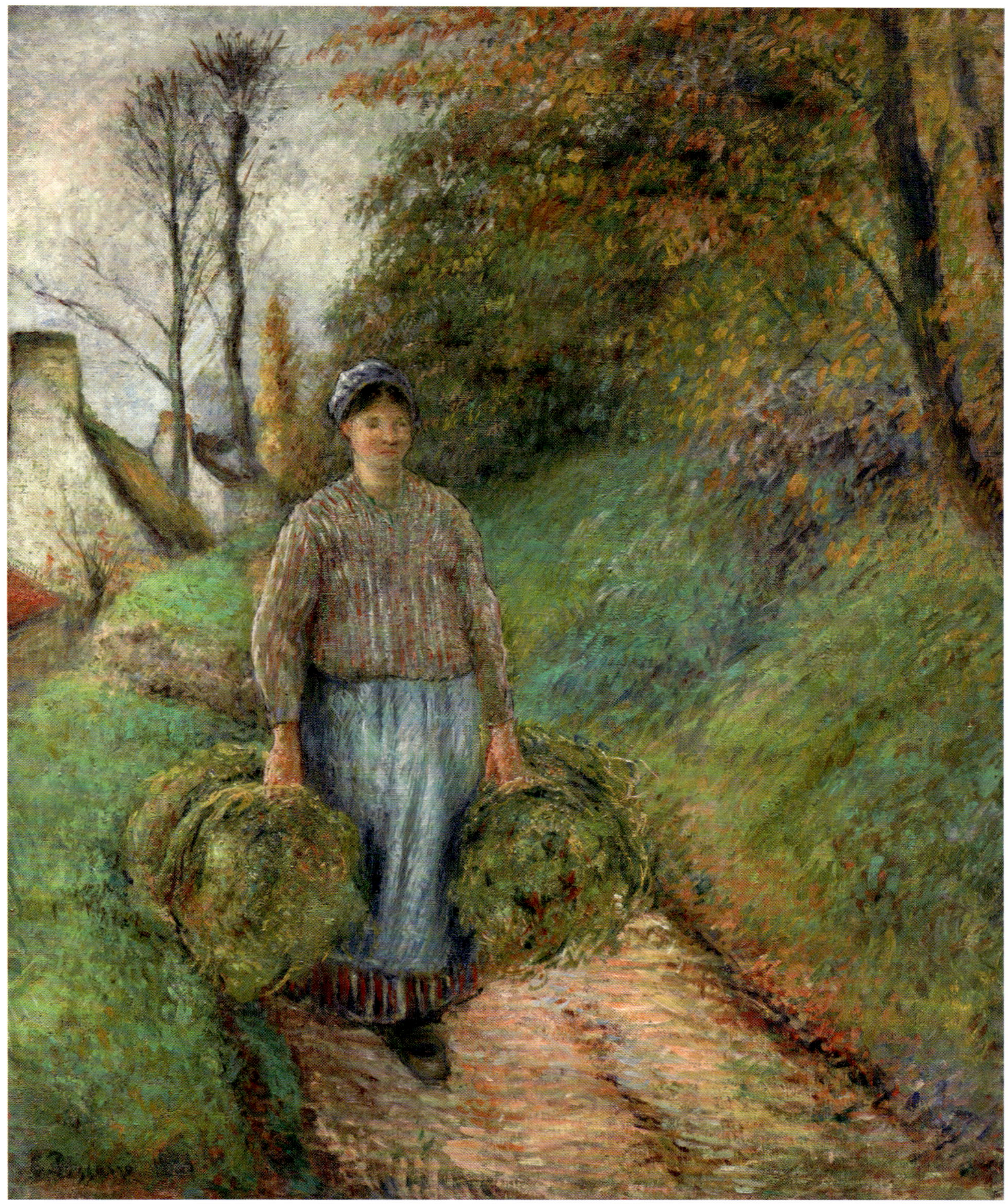

CAT. 24

Camille Pissarro
(born in Charlotte Amalie, Danish West Indies (present-day U.S. Virgin Islands), 1830–
died in Paris, France, 1903)

Peasant Woman Carrying Two Bundles of Hay
1883
Oil on canvas, 29 × 24 in. (73.7 × 61.0 cm)
Dallas Museum of Art, gift of the Meadows Foundation, Incorporated, 1981.132

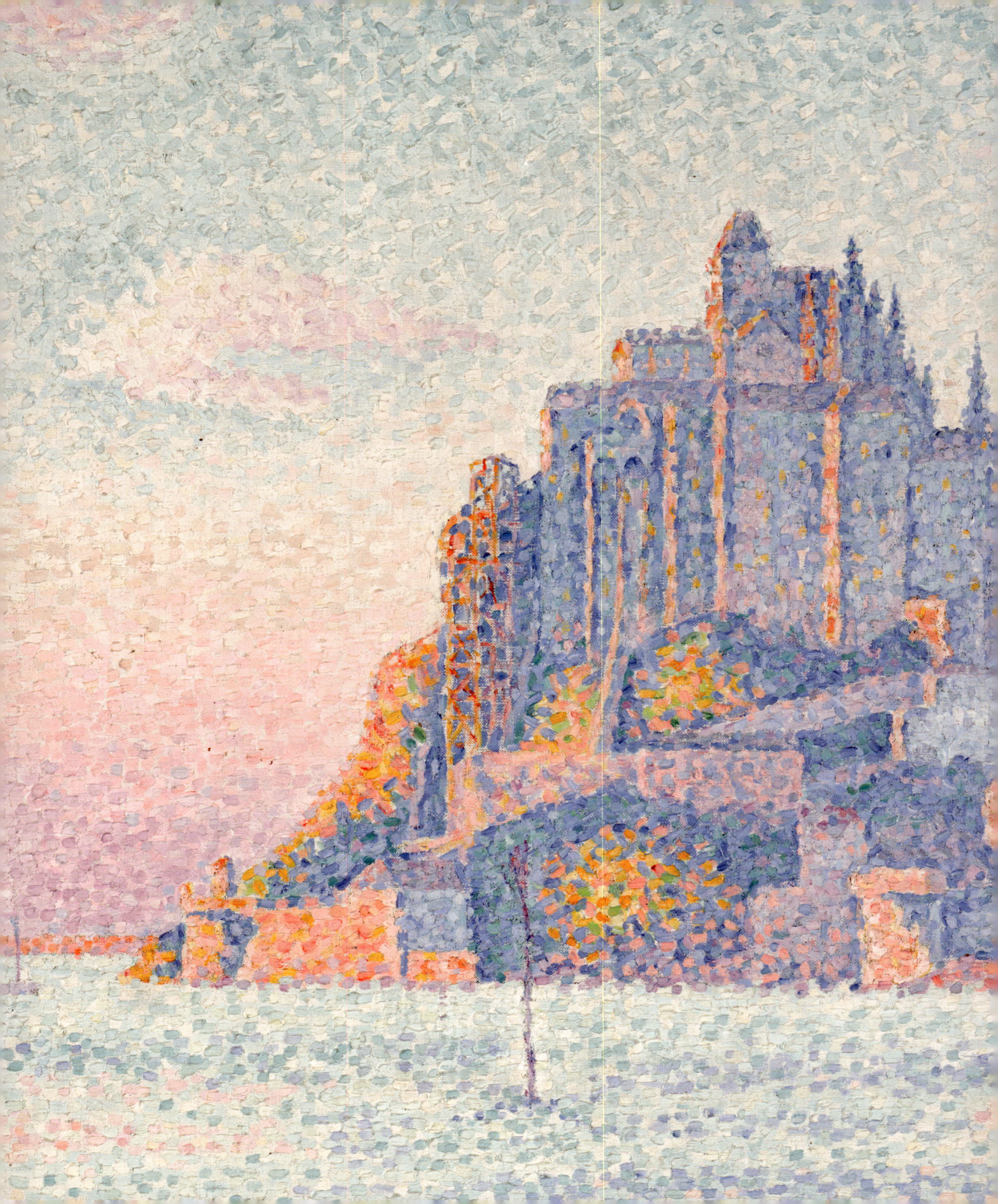

Weird Science

GEORGES SEURAT revealed the shocking new style he invented, and kept secret, in his monumental painting *A Sunday on La Grande Jatte—1884* (1884–1886, Art Institute of Chicago). Whereas the Impressionists explored color and optical theories intuitively, Seurat transformed them into a science. The result was a technique he called Chromo-Luminarism, which is better known today as Pointillism or Neo-Impressionism. Instead of mixing colors on his palette, Seurat placed individual points of brilliant color side by side that, when seen from a distance, blend in the viewer's eyes. He aimed to create a truer representation of how we optically experience light and, in the process, restore the compositional stability that many felt had been abandoned by the Impressionists' emphasis on spontaneity.

Seurat's debut of Pointillism at what would be the last Impressionist show in 1886 provoked ridicule from critics and confounded exhibition-goers. Within the Impressionist circle, artists were split. Many saw the potential and experimented with the style, but most moved on quickly from its slow and laborious technique. Still others saw it as the death knell of Impressionism and left Paris in search of a new direction for modern art.

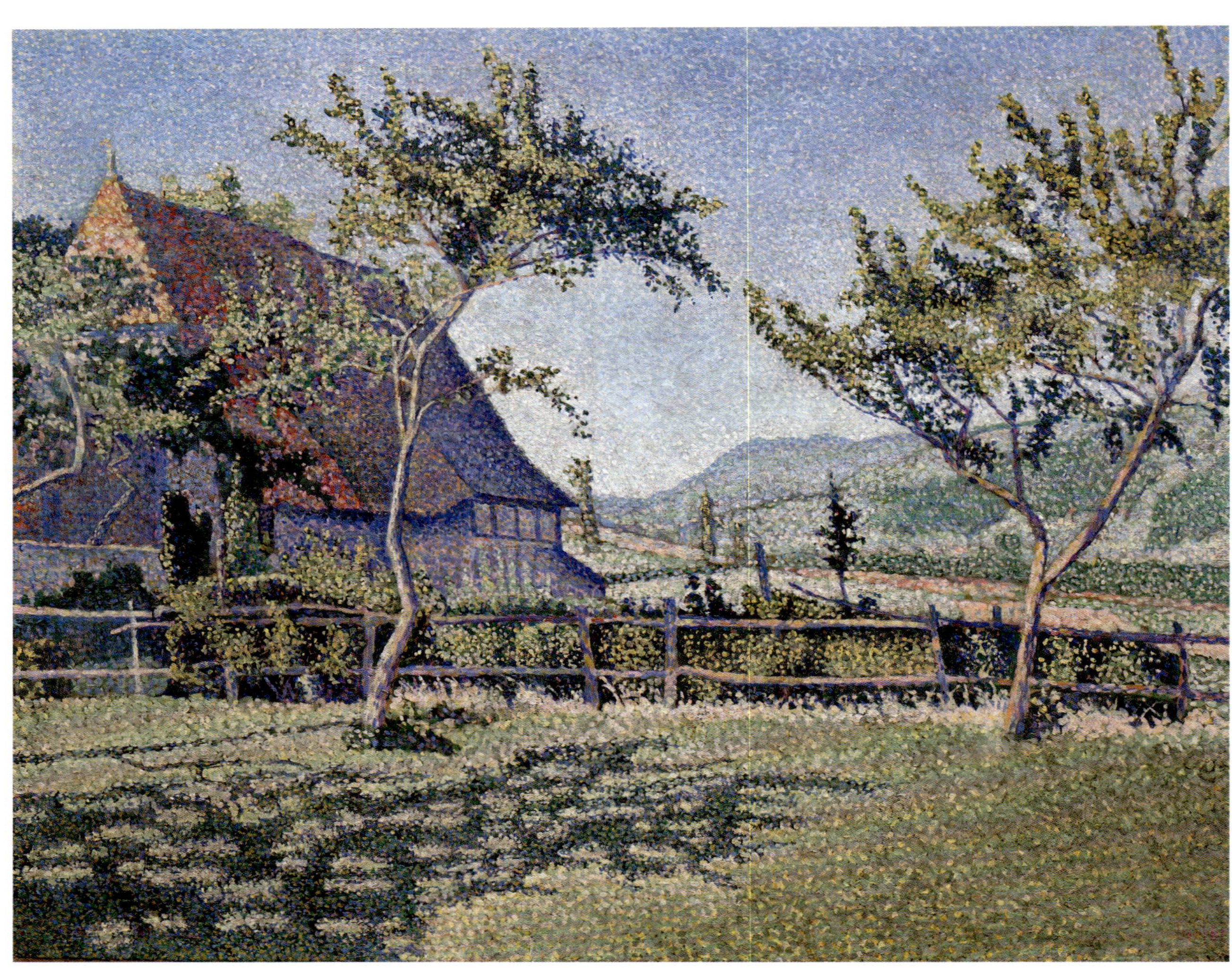

CAT. 25

Paul Signac
(born in Paris, France, 1863–died in Paris, France, 1935)
Comblat-le-Château, the Meadow (Le Pré), Opus 161
1887
Oil on canvas, 26 ⅛ × 32 ½ in. (66.4 × 82.6 cm)
Dallas Museum of Art, The Eugene and Margaret McDermott Art Fund, Inc.,
in honor of Bonnie Pitman, 2010.14.McD

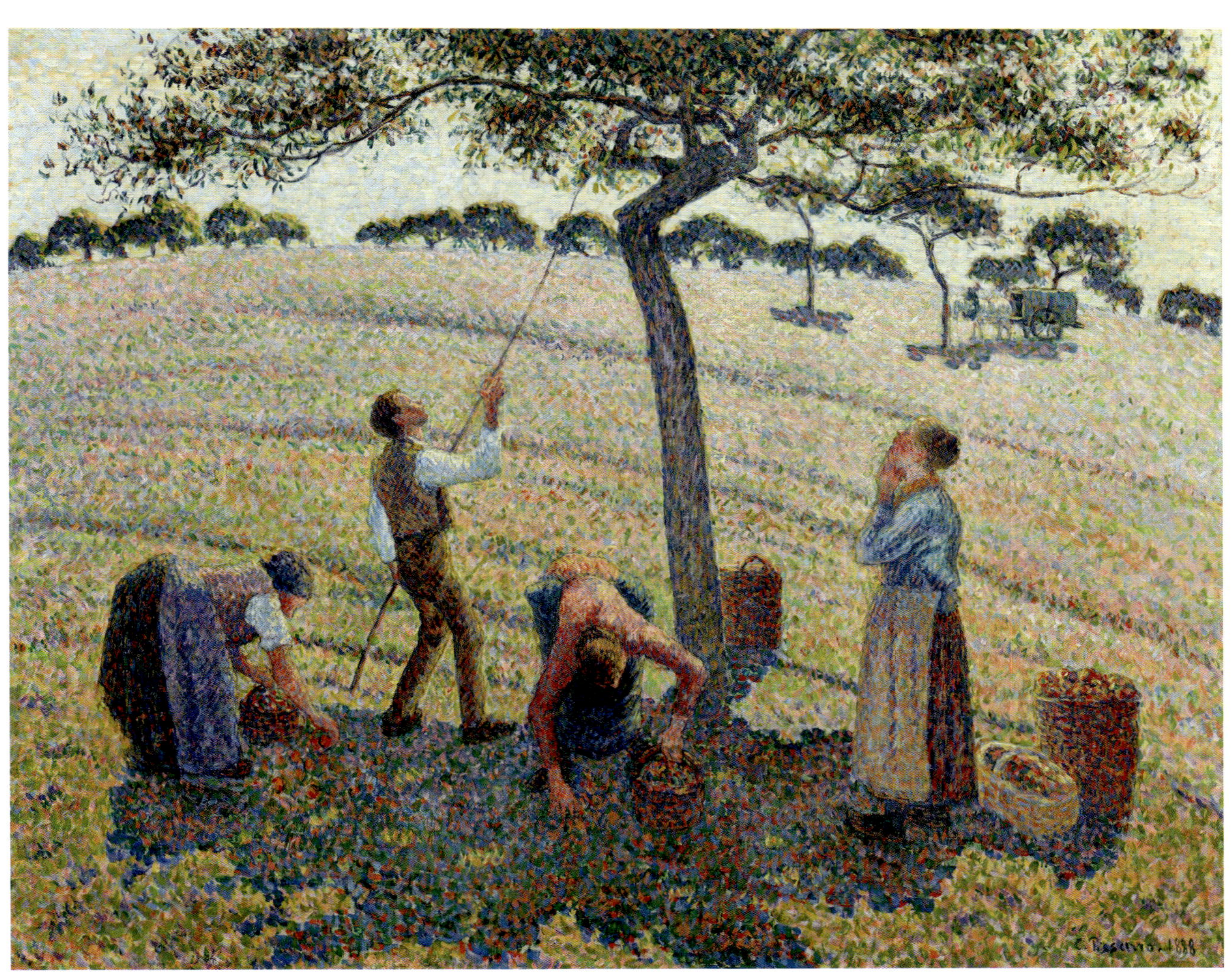

CAT. 26

Camille Pissarro
(born in Charlotte Amalie, Danish West Indies (present-day U.S. Virgin Islands), 1830–
died in Paris, France, 1903)

Apple Harvest
1888
Oil on canvas, 24 x 29 ⅛ in. (61.0 x 74.0 cm)
Dallas Museum of Art, Munger Fund, 1955.17.M

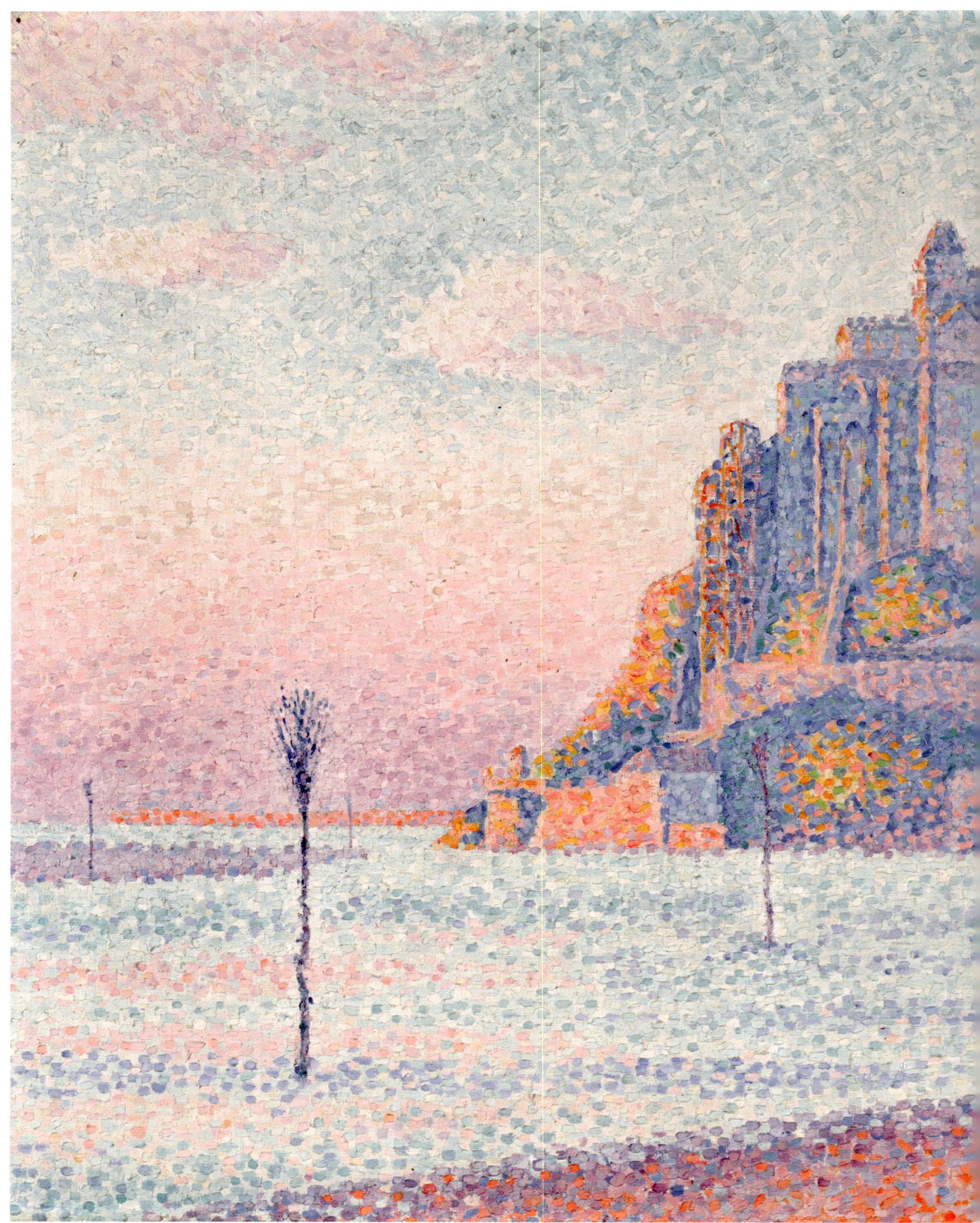

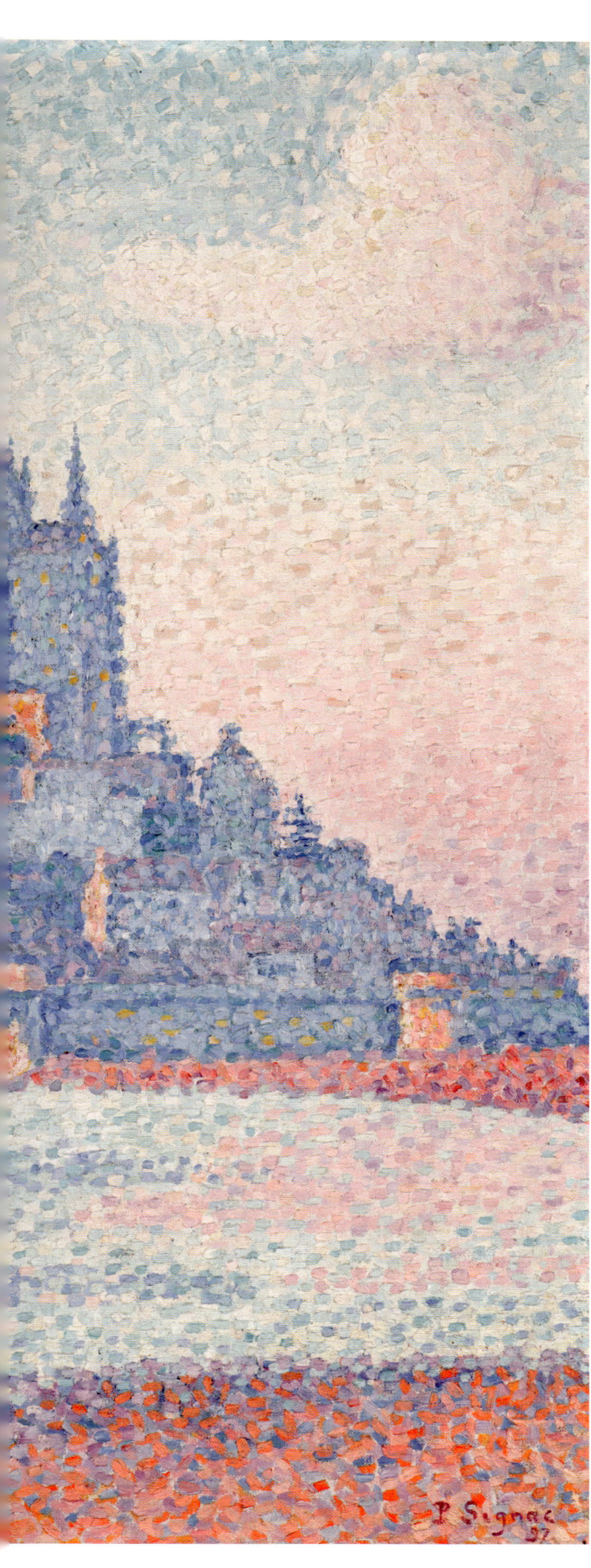

CAT. 27

Paul Signac
(born in Paris, France, 1863–died in Paris, France, 1935)
Mont Saint-Michel, Setting Sun
1897
Oil on canvas, 26 × 32 ⅛ in. (66.0 × 81.6 cm)
Dallas Museum of Art, The Eugene and Margaret McDermott Art Fund, Inc.,
bequest of Mrs. Eugene McDermott in honor of Bill Booziotis, 2019.67.25.McD

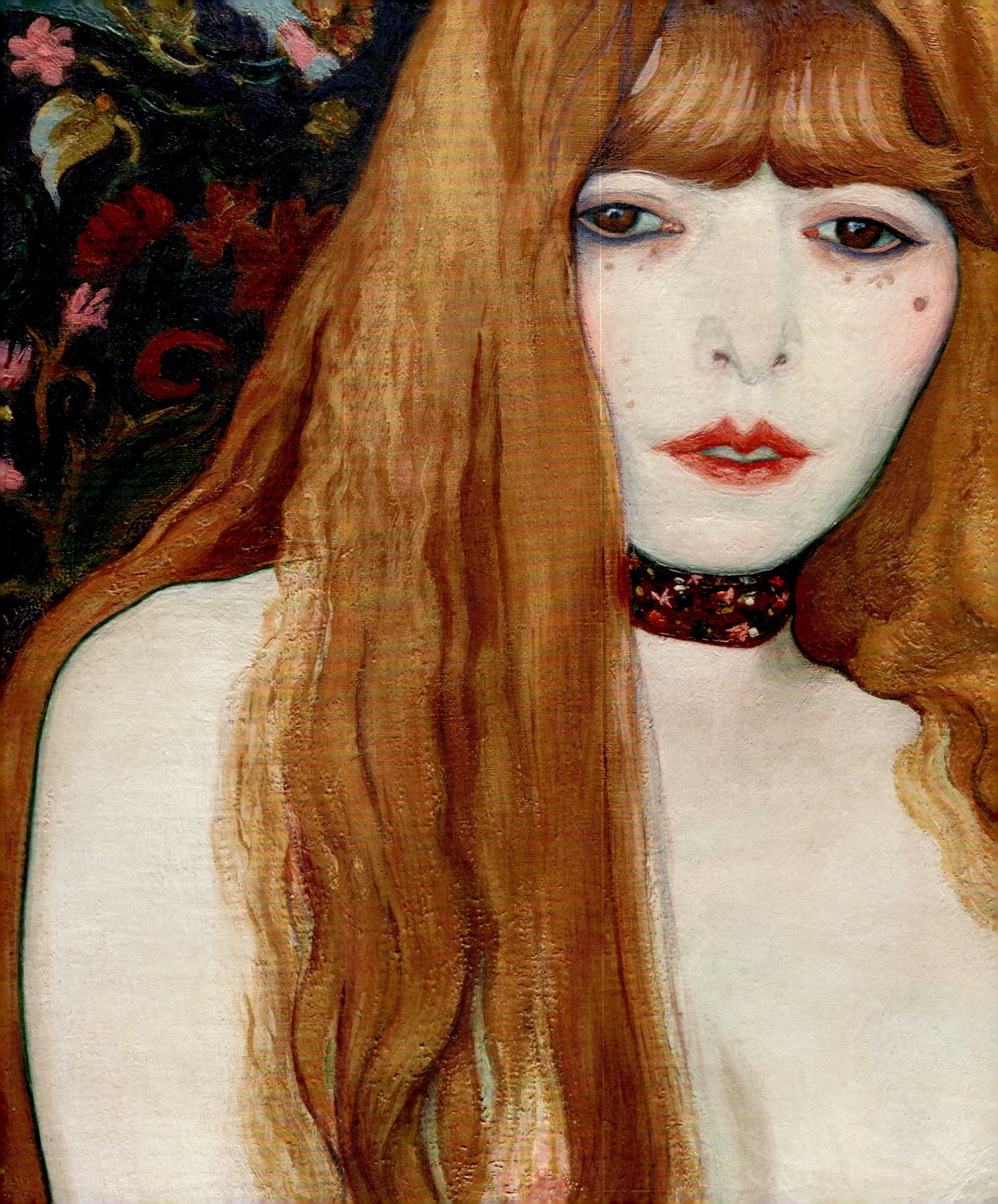

Side Effects

GEORGES SEURAT'S debut of Pointillism in 1886 created a backlash within the avant-garde. Many with roots in Impressionism, including Paul Cézanne, Vincent van Gogh, and Paul Gauguin, led a younger generation of artists in developing new styles that prioritized emotions, ideas, and personal expression over purely optical impressions. Antinaturalistic colors, exaggerated forms, and symbolic subjects characterize the production of the artists we now call Post-Impressionists.

Although aspects of his theories and lifestyle are problematic, Gauguin was instrumental in this shift. He sought to restore a sense of authenticity to art making by stripping away Western pictorial conventions such as linear perspective and modeling. He left Paris in search of "uncivilized" subjects, first in France's remote regions and later in its colonies, that would embody the "primitive" quality he sought in his art. Van Gogh, Emile Bernard, and Paul Sérusier are among those who followed this example.

The Synthetic style Gauguin developed with Bernard, which emphasized the role of memory, imagination, and abstraction, would have a profound impact on Van Gogh and the young group of artists who called themselves The Nabis (Prophets) in the late 1880s. The latter embraced the subversive concept that a painting was nothing more than a decorative arrangement of colors on a flat surface.

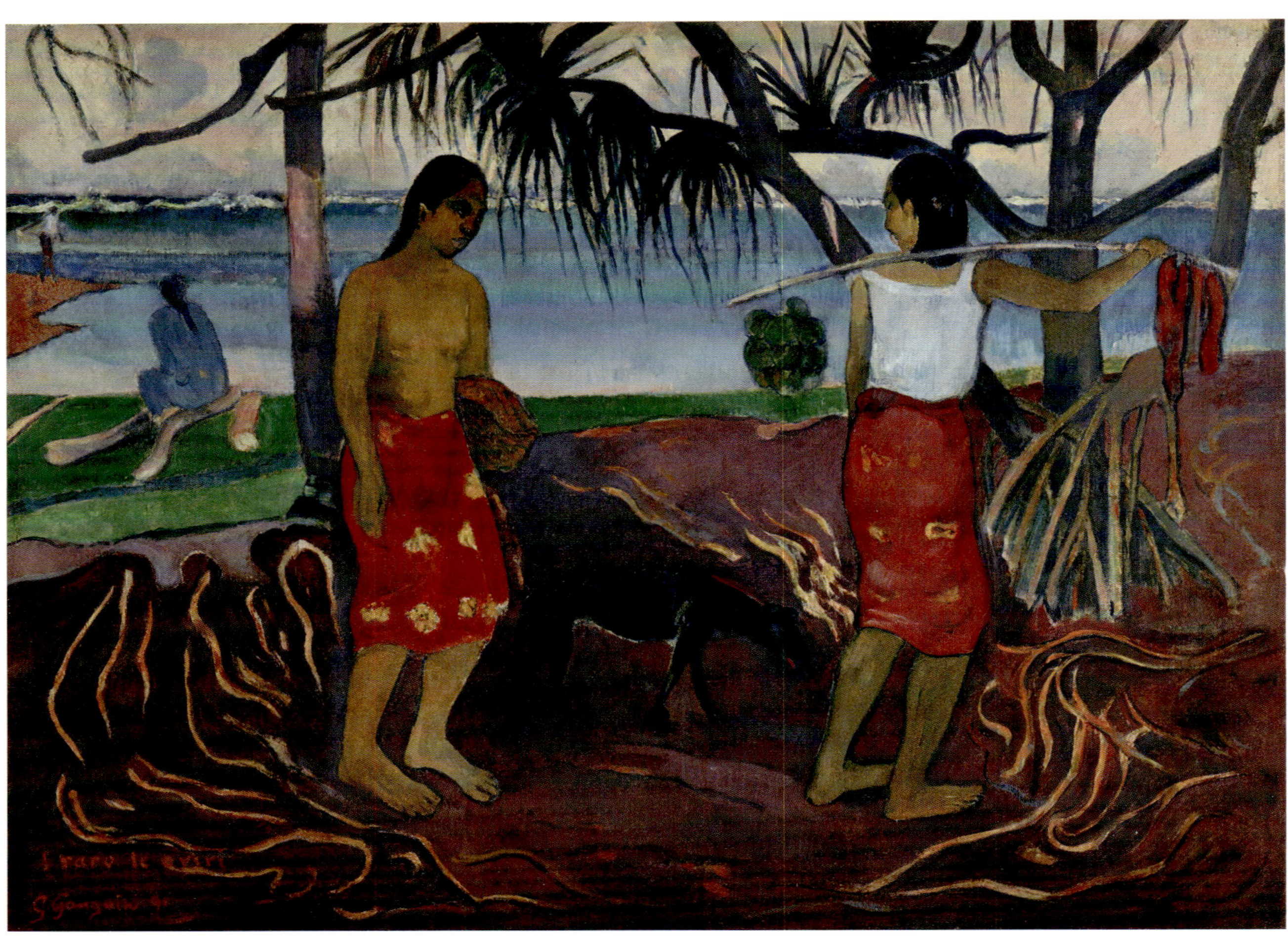

CAT. 28

Paul Gauguin
(born in Paris, France, 1848–died in Atuona, Hiva Oa, French Polynesia, 1903)
I Raro te Oviri (Under the Pandanus)
1891
Oil on canvas, 26 ½ x 35 ¾ in. (67.3 x 90.8 cm)
Dallas Museum of Art, Foundation for the Arts Collection, gift of the
Adele R. Levy Fund, Inc., 1963.58.FA

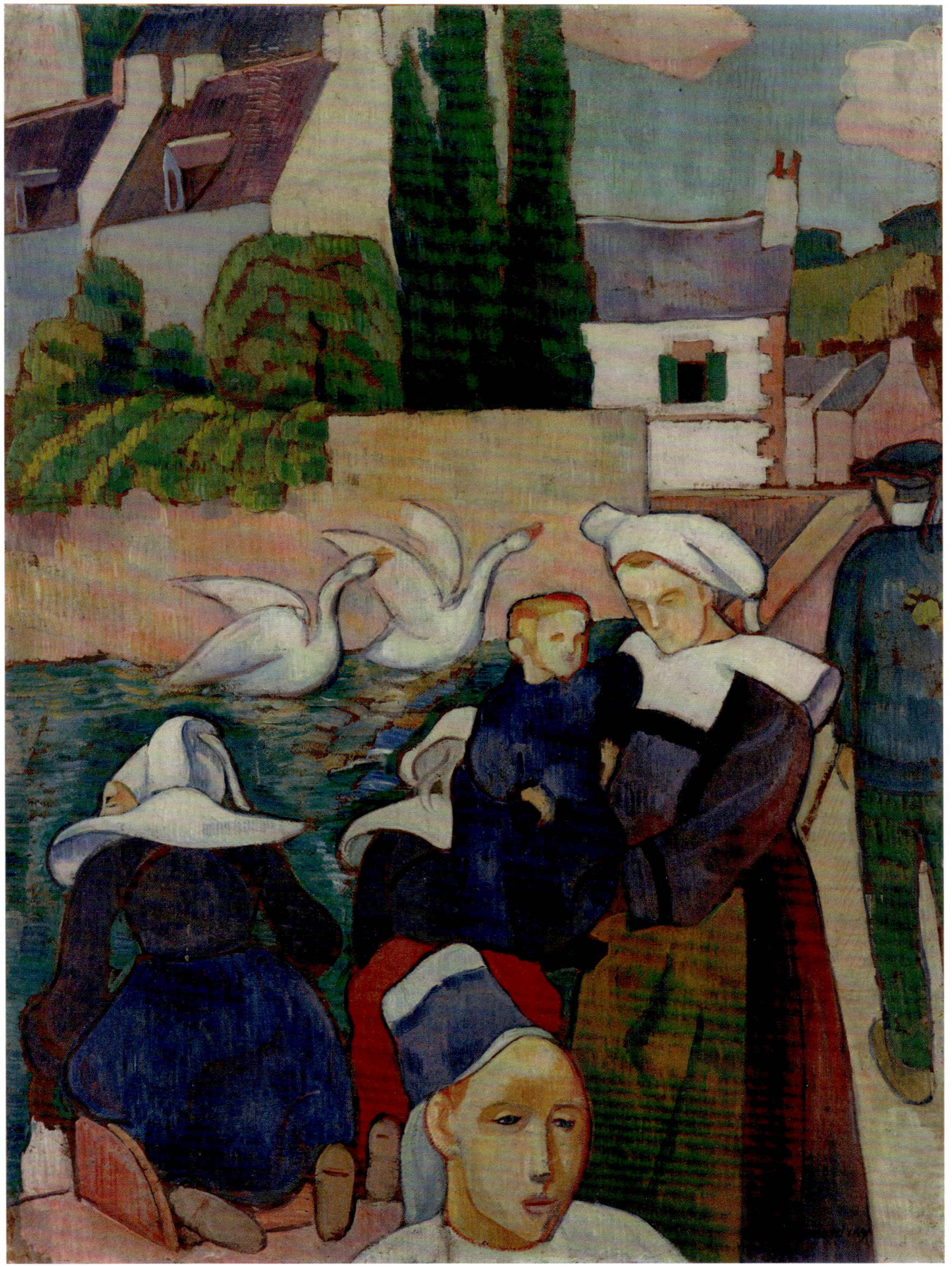

CAT. 29

Emile Bernard
(born in Lille, France, 1868–died in Paris, France, 1941)

Bridge at Pont Aven
1891
Oil on canvas, 45 ½ × 32 ½ in. (115.6 × 82.6 cm)
Dallas Museum of Art, gift of the Estate of Ina MacNaughton, 1992.27

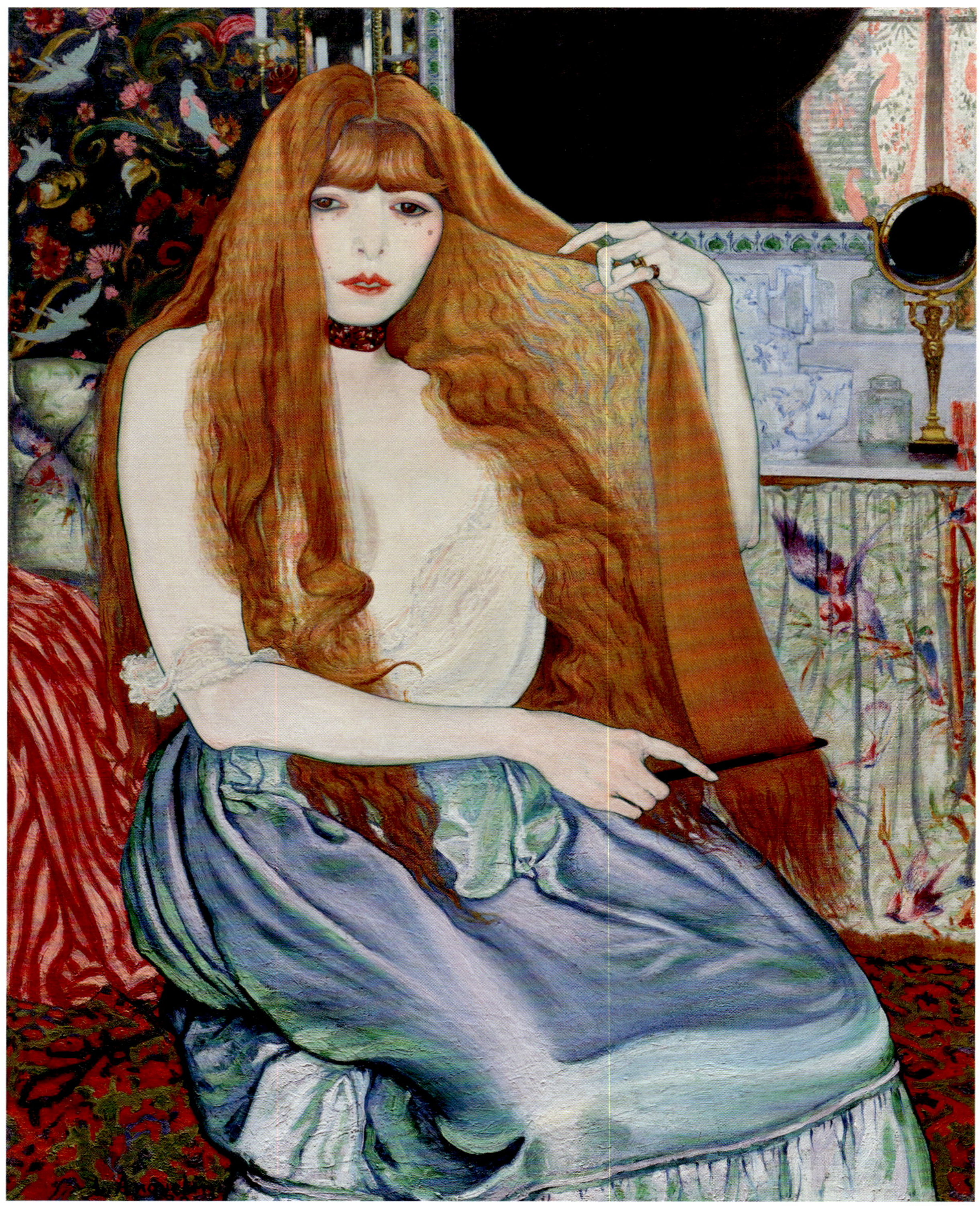

CAT. 30

Louis Anquetin
(born in Étrépagny, France, 1861–died in Paris, France, 1932)
Woman at Her Toilette
1889
Oil on canvas, 36 ¼ × 28 ¾ in. (92.1 × 73.0 cm)
Dallas Museum of Art, Foundation for the Arts Collection,
Mrs. John B. O'Hara Fund, 2020.3.FA

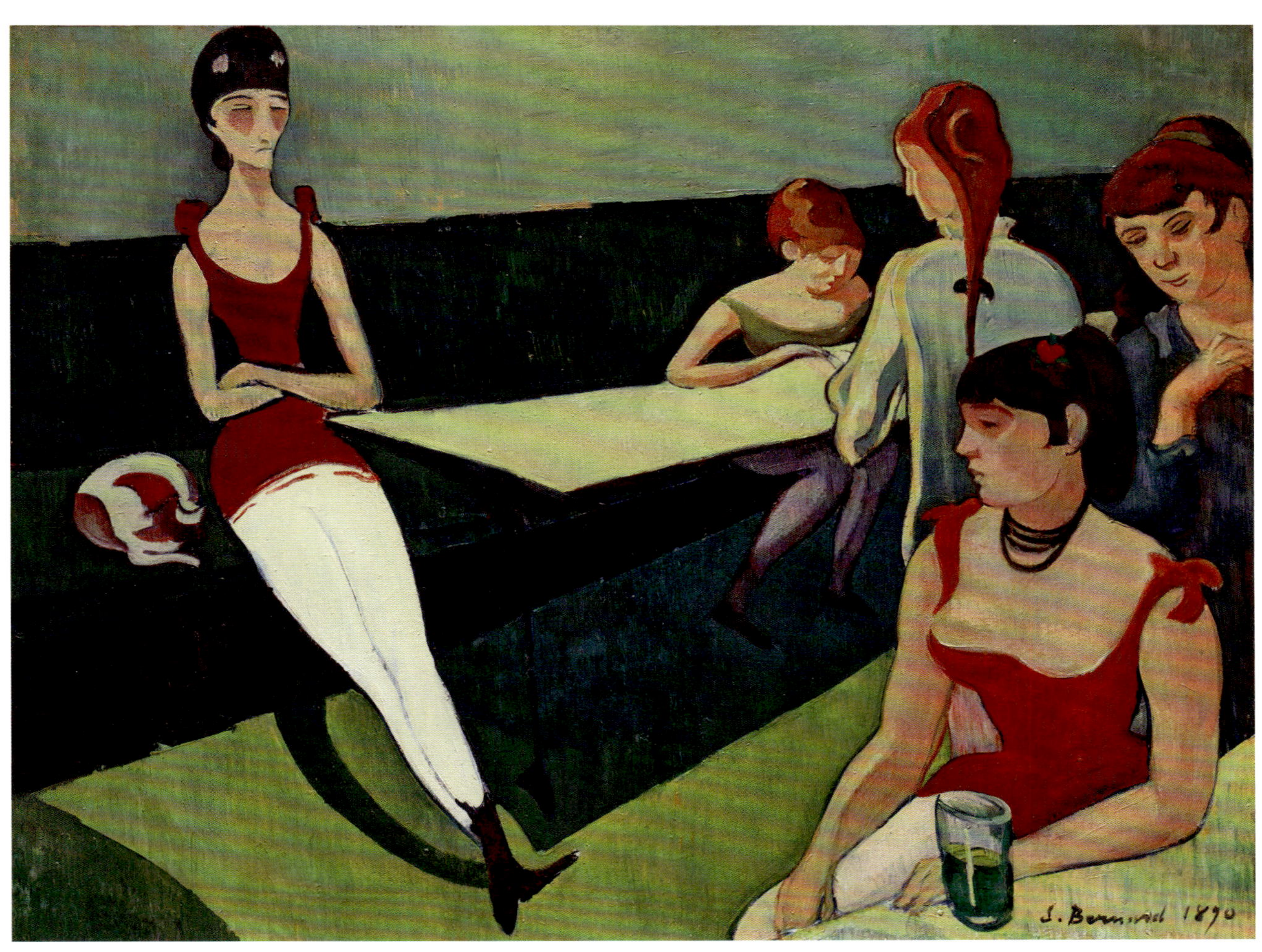

CAT. 31

Emile Bernard
(born in Lille, France, 1868–died in Paris, France, 1941)
The Salon
1890
Oil on canvas, 35 ⅛ × 45 ⅞ in. (89.2 × 116.5 cm)
Dallas Museum of Art, The Eugene and Margaret McDermott
Art Fund, Inc., 2018.4.McD

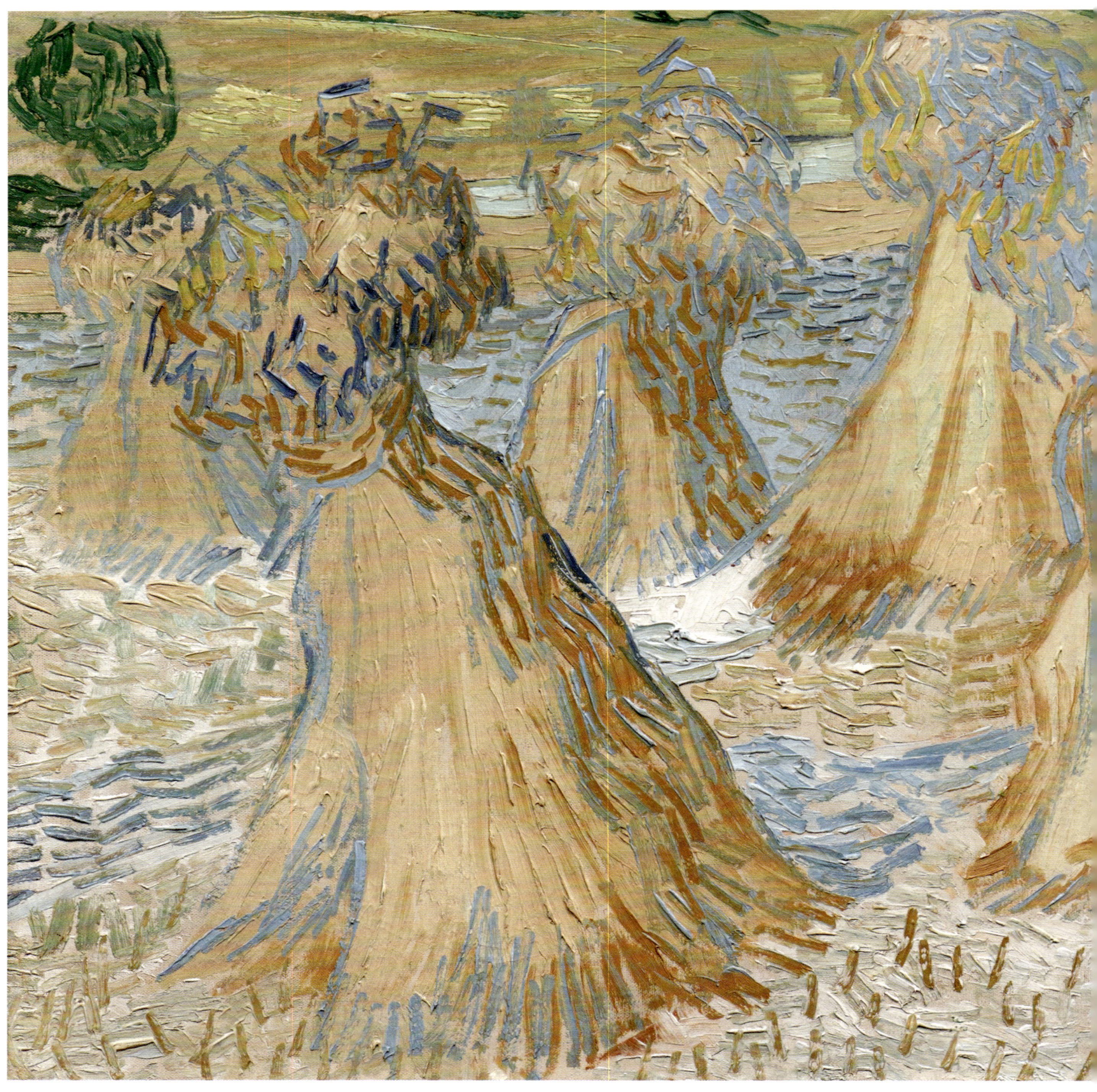

CAT. 32

Vincent van Gogh
(born in Zundert, Netherlands, 1853–died in Auvers-sur-Oise, France, 1890)
Sheaves of Wheat
1890
Oil on canvas, 20 × 40 in. (50.8 × 101.6 cm)
Dallas Museum of Art, The Wendy and Emery Reves Collection, 1985.R.80

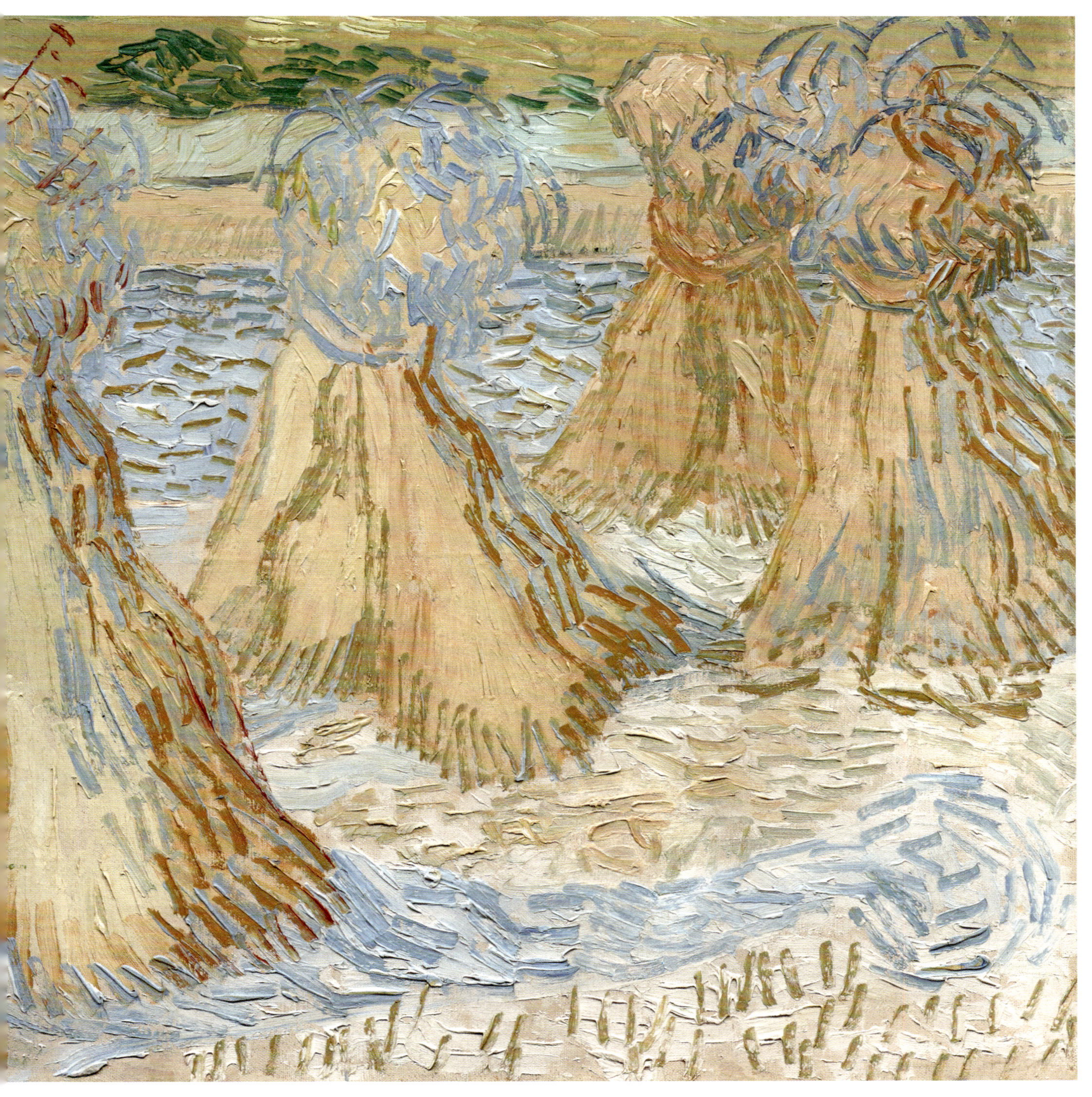

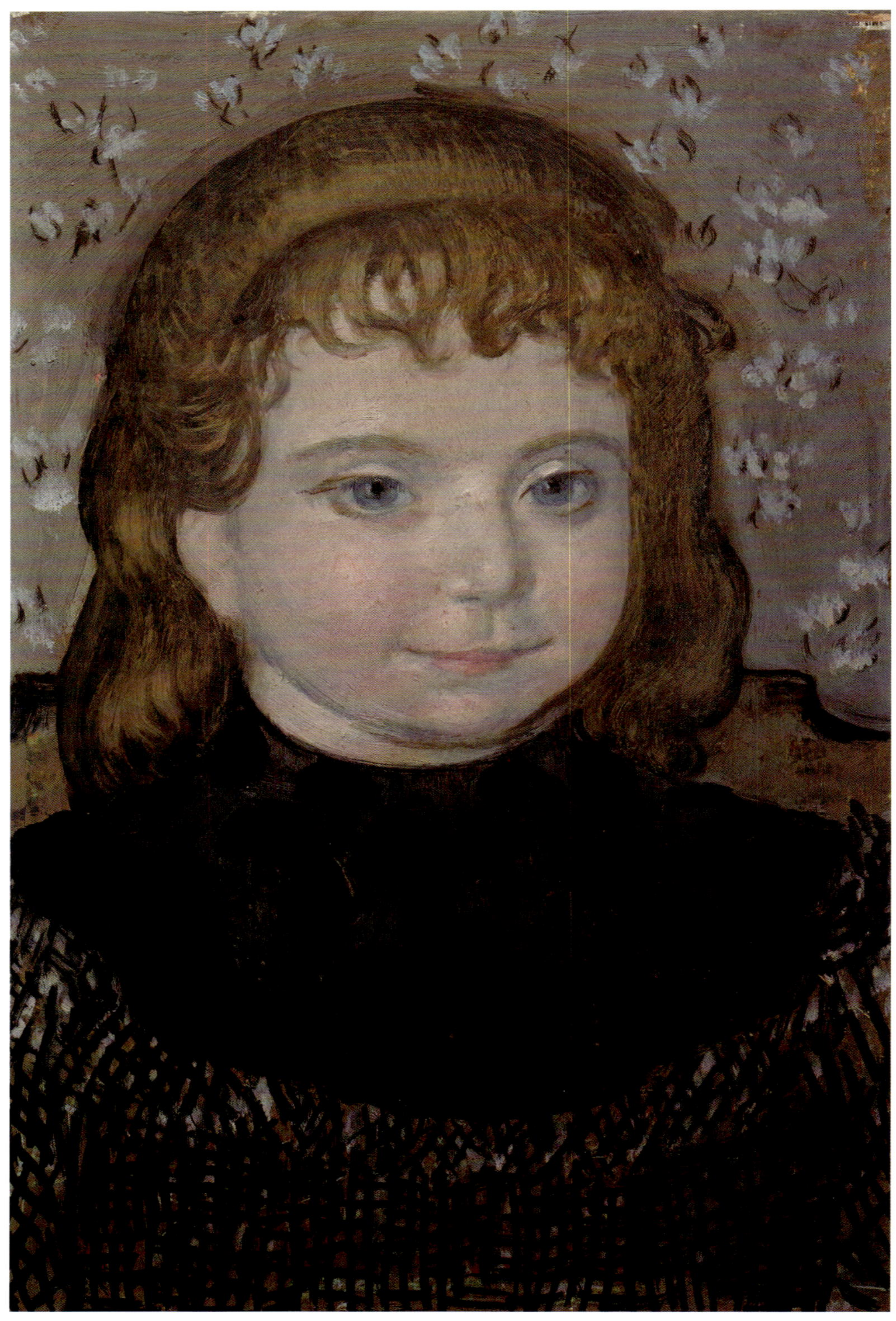

CAT. 33

Maurice Denis
(born in Granville, France, 1870–died in Paris, France, 1943)

Portrait of a Young Girl (Thérèse Watillaux)
1896
Oil on cardboard, 15 ¾ × 10 ⅜ in. (40.0 × 26.4 cm)
Dallas Museum of Art, Beatrice and Patrick Haggerty Acquisition Fund, gift
of Lawrence Milton Davis by exchange, gift of Caren Prothro by exchange, and
the Patsy Lacy Griffith Collection, gift of Patsy Lacy Griffith by exchange, 2014.27

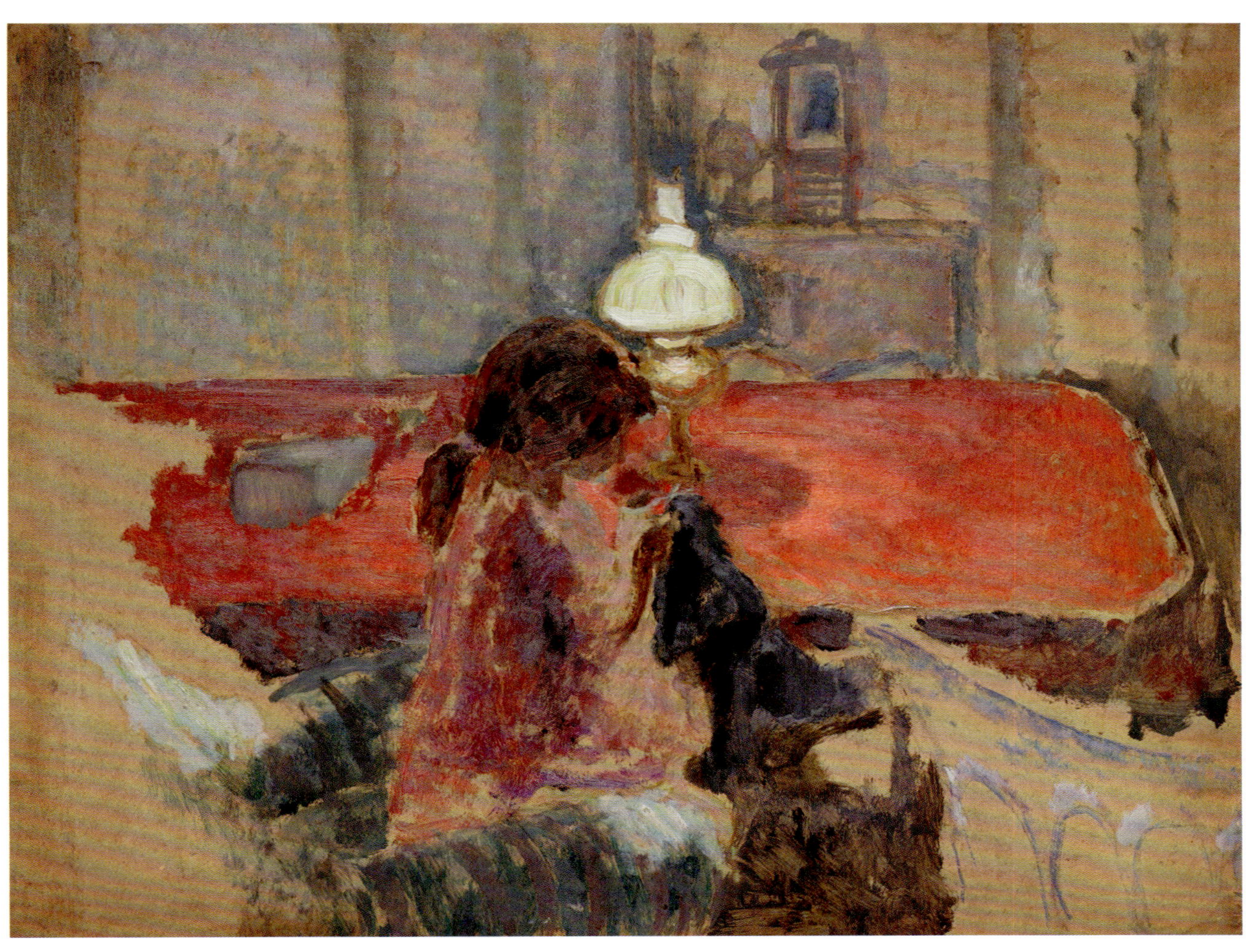

CAT. 34

Pierre Bonnard
(born in Fontenay-aux-Roses, France, 1867–died in Le Cannet, France, 1947)
Woman with a Lamp
1909
Oil on paper mounted on canvas, 19 ½ × 25 ¼ in. (49.5 × 64.1 cm)
Dallas Museum of Art, gift of Ann Jacobus Folz, 2017.44.2

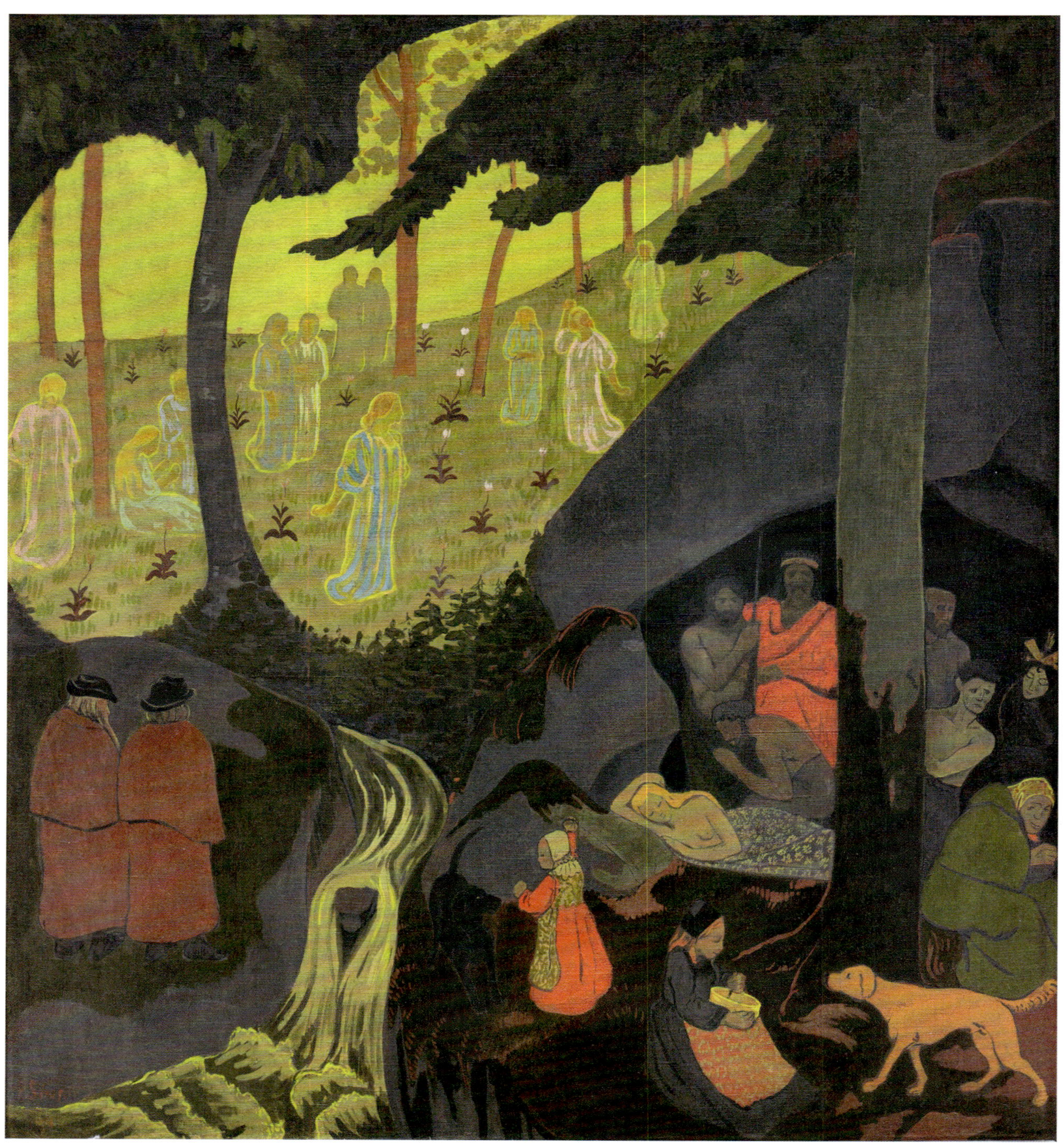

CAT. 35

Paul Sérusier
(born in Paris, France, 1864–died in Morlaix, France, 1927)
Celtic Tale
1894
Oil on canvas, 43 ⅞ × 44 in. (111.4 × 111.7 cm)
Dallas Museum of Art, Foundation for the Arts Collection,
gift of Mr. and Mrs. Frederick Mayer, 1983.52.FA

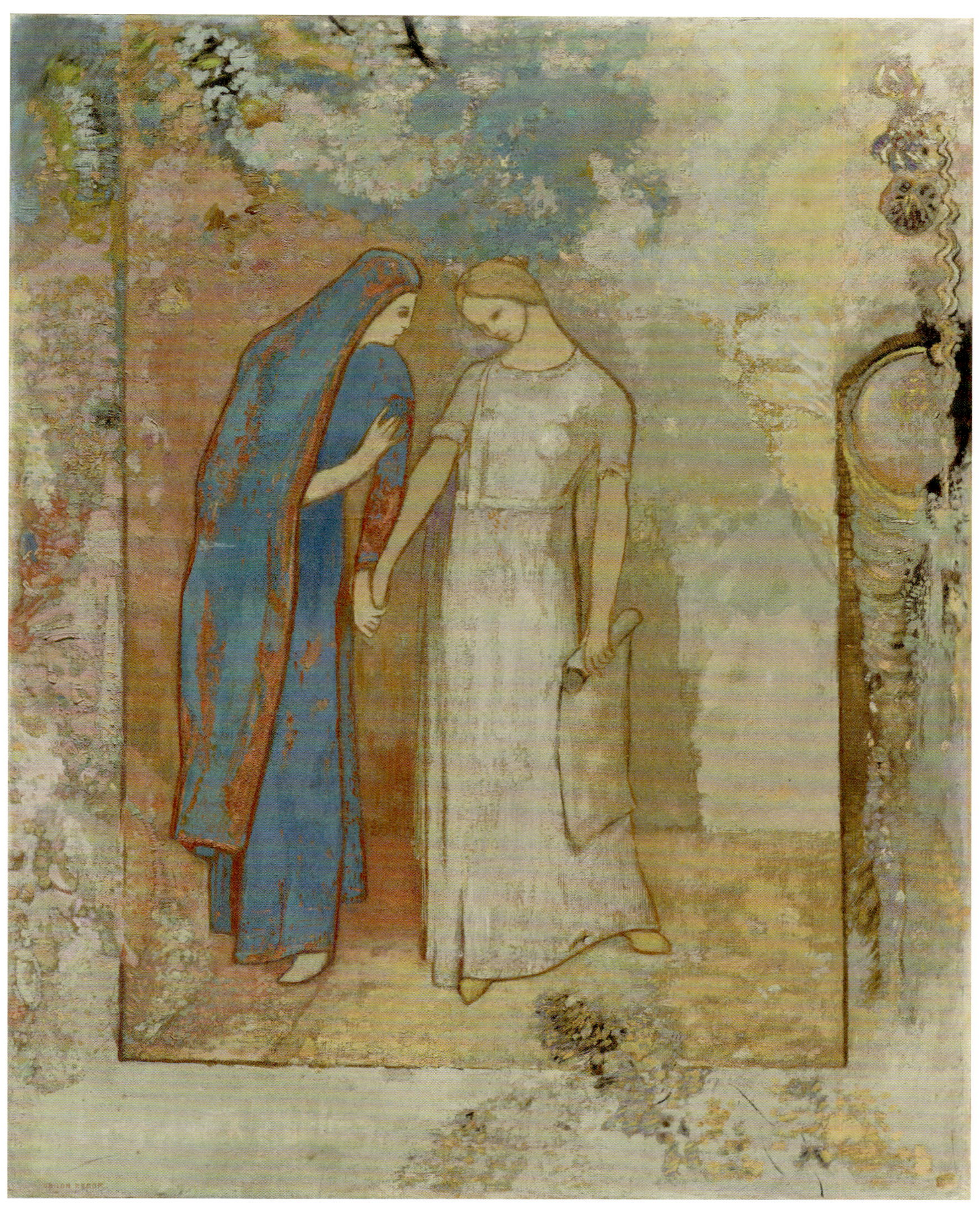

CAT. 36

Odilon Redon
(born in Bordeaux, France, 1840–died in Paris, France, 1916)
Initiation to Study—Two Young Ladies
c. 1905
Oil on canvas, 37 × 29 ⅜ in. (94.0 × 74.6 cm)
Dallas Museum of Art, Foundation for the Arts Collection,
anonymous gift, 1963.80.FA

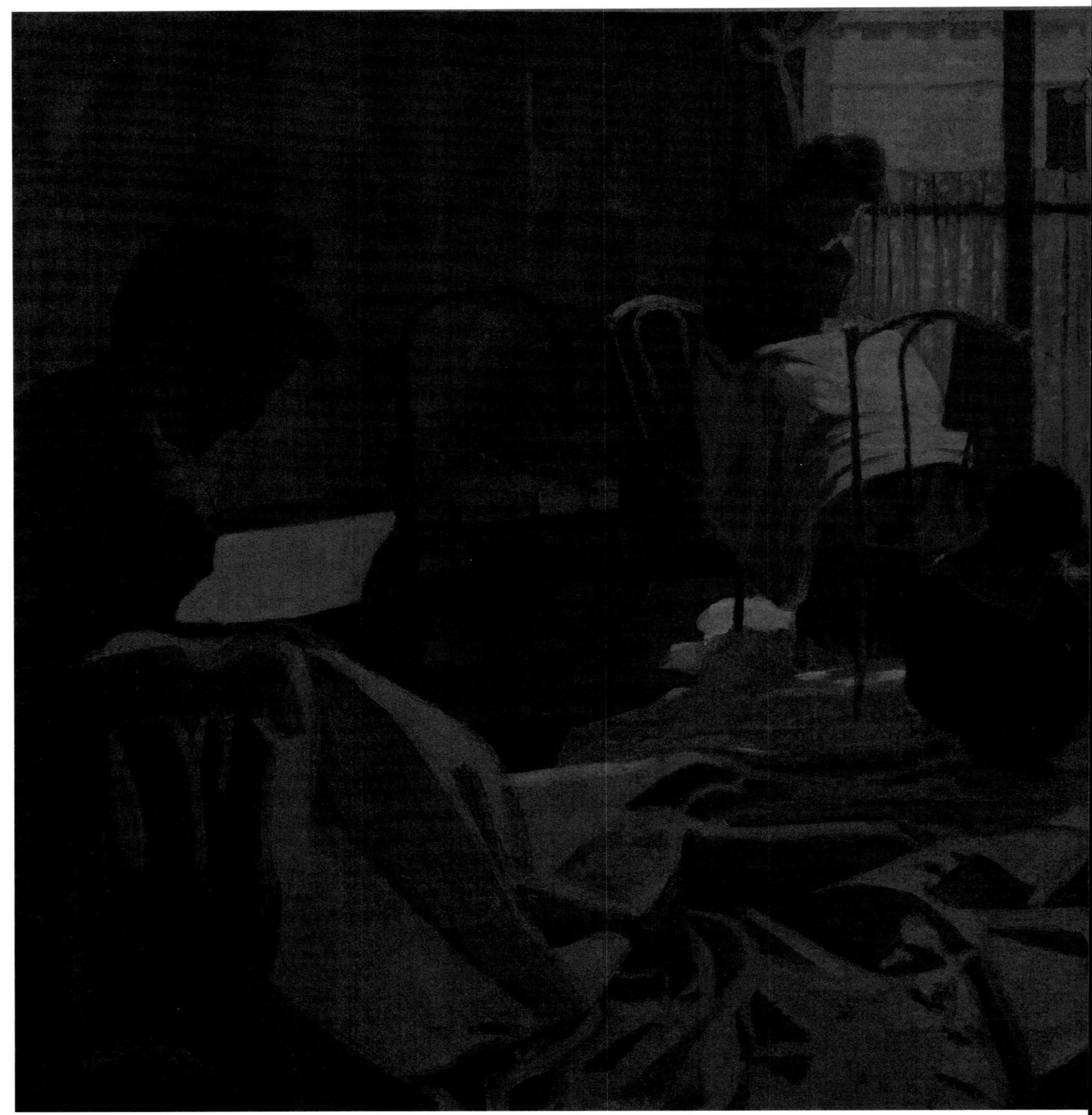

CAT. 37

Félix Vallotton
(born in Lausanne, Switzerland, 1865–died in Neuilly-sur-Seine, France, 1925)
The Laundress, Blue Room
1900
Tempera on cardboard mounted on canvas, 19 ¾ × 31 ¼ in. (50.2 × 79.4 cm)
Dallas Museum of Art, Foundation for the Arts Collection, Mrs. John B. O'Hara
Fund in honor of Mrs. Alfred L. Bromberg, 1996.48.FA

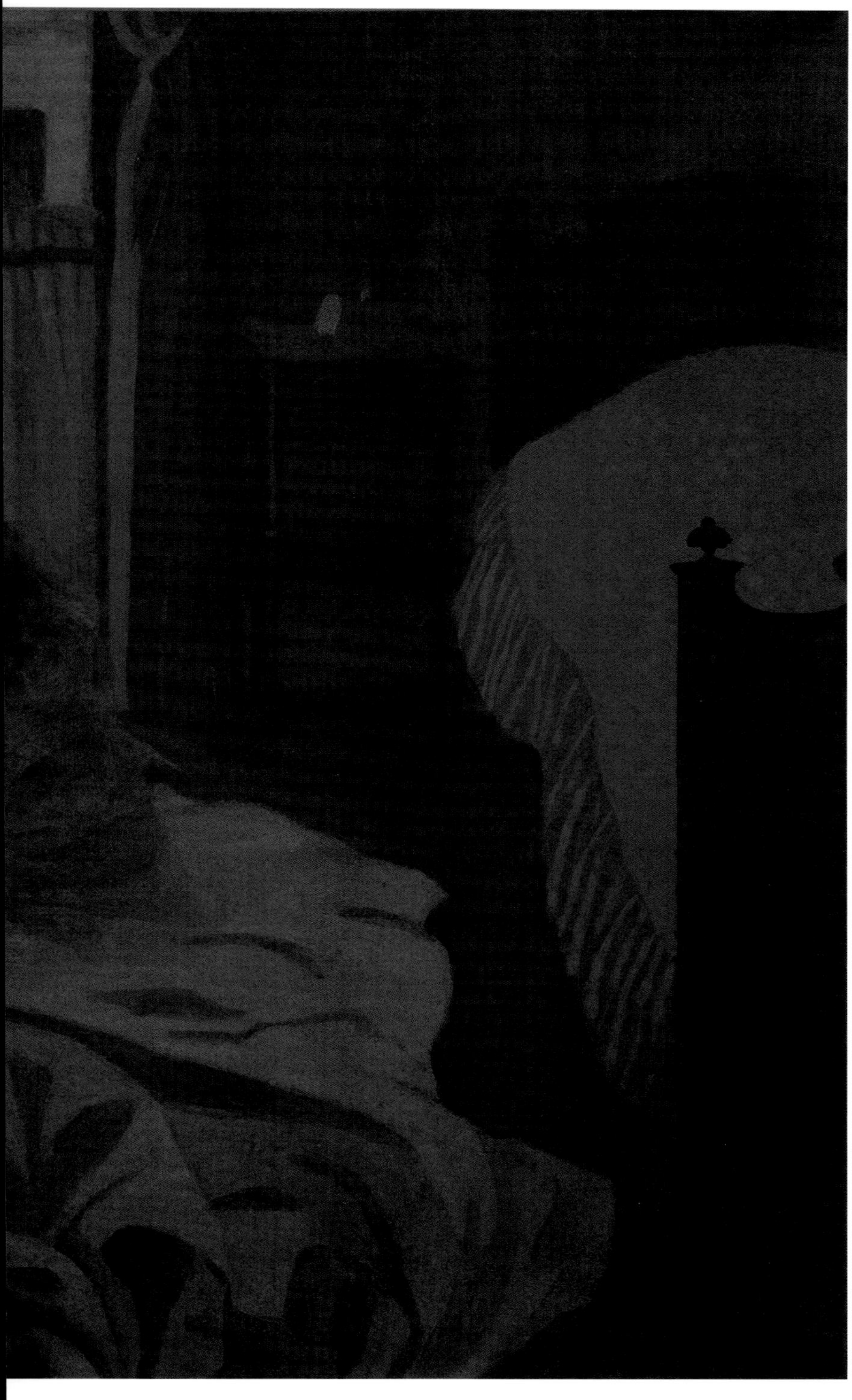

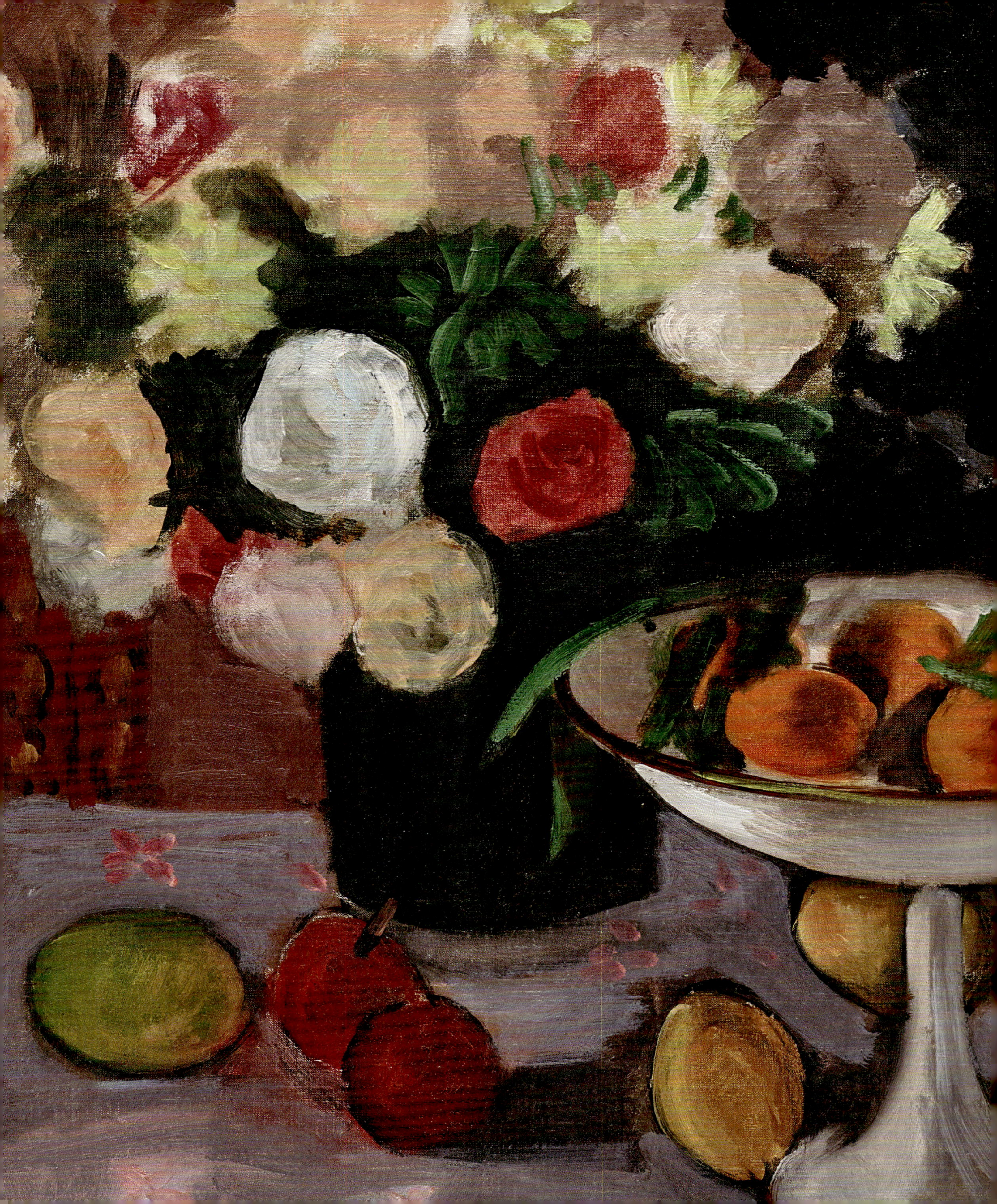

Ever After

THE RADICAL AESTHETICS and groundbreaking subjects launched by the Impressionists and the Post-Impressionists who followed set the trajectory for the development of contemporary art in the twentieth century. Large retrospectives of the work of Pierre-Auguste Renoir, Paul Cézanne, Vincent van Gogh, and Paul Gauguin held in Paris, Amsterdam, Vienna, Dresden, and Berlin in the first decade of the 1900s contributed to the dissemination of their collective styles and theories across Europe. Younger generations of avant-garde artists actively engaged with the movements' core tenets, whether directly or indirectly, whether adopting or rejecting them.

Almost every stylistic breakthrough from this period—Cubism, Fauvism, Expressionism, Futurism, Abstraction—had its roots in the Impressionists' subversion of traditional Academic values, from the subject depicted to the finish of the brightly colored surface. The works featured in this epilogue of sorts by Piet Mondrian, Edvard Munch, Ernst Ludwig Kirchner, Alexei Jawlensky, André Derain, Pierre Bonnard, and Henri Matisse offer tantalizing glimpses into some of these innovative movements and their continuation, often to brilliant ends, of Impressionism's legacy.

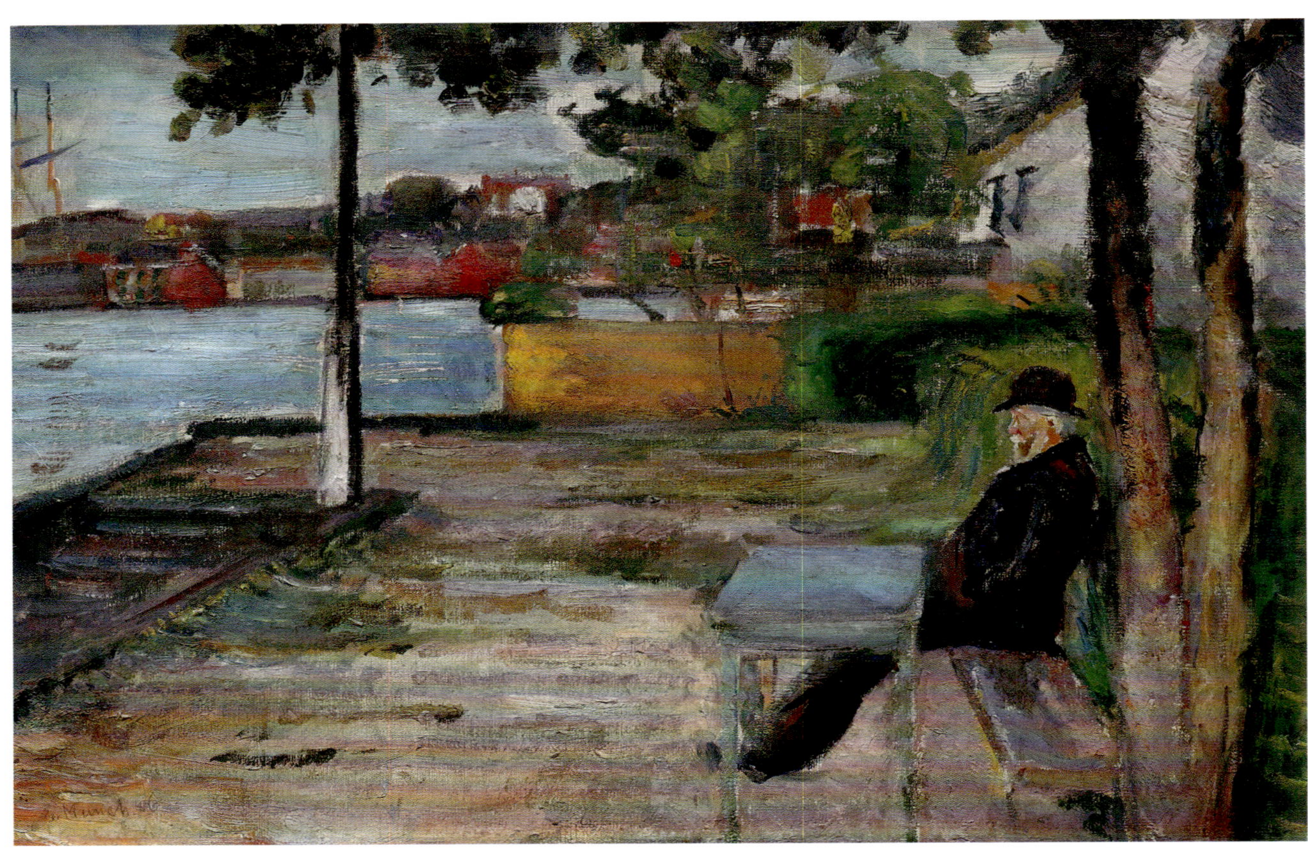

CAT. 38

Edvard Munch
(born in Ådalsbruk, Norway, 1863–died in Oslo, Norway, 1944)
View from Hisøya Near Arendal
1886
Oil on canvas, 16 ¼ × 24 ⅝ in. (41.3 × 62.6 cm)
Dallas Museum of Art, gift of Cornelia and Ralph Heins in honor
of Elinor Heins, 2021.32.12

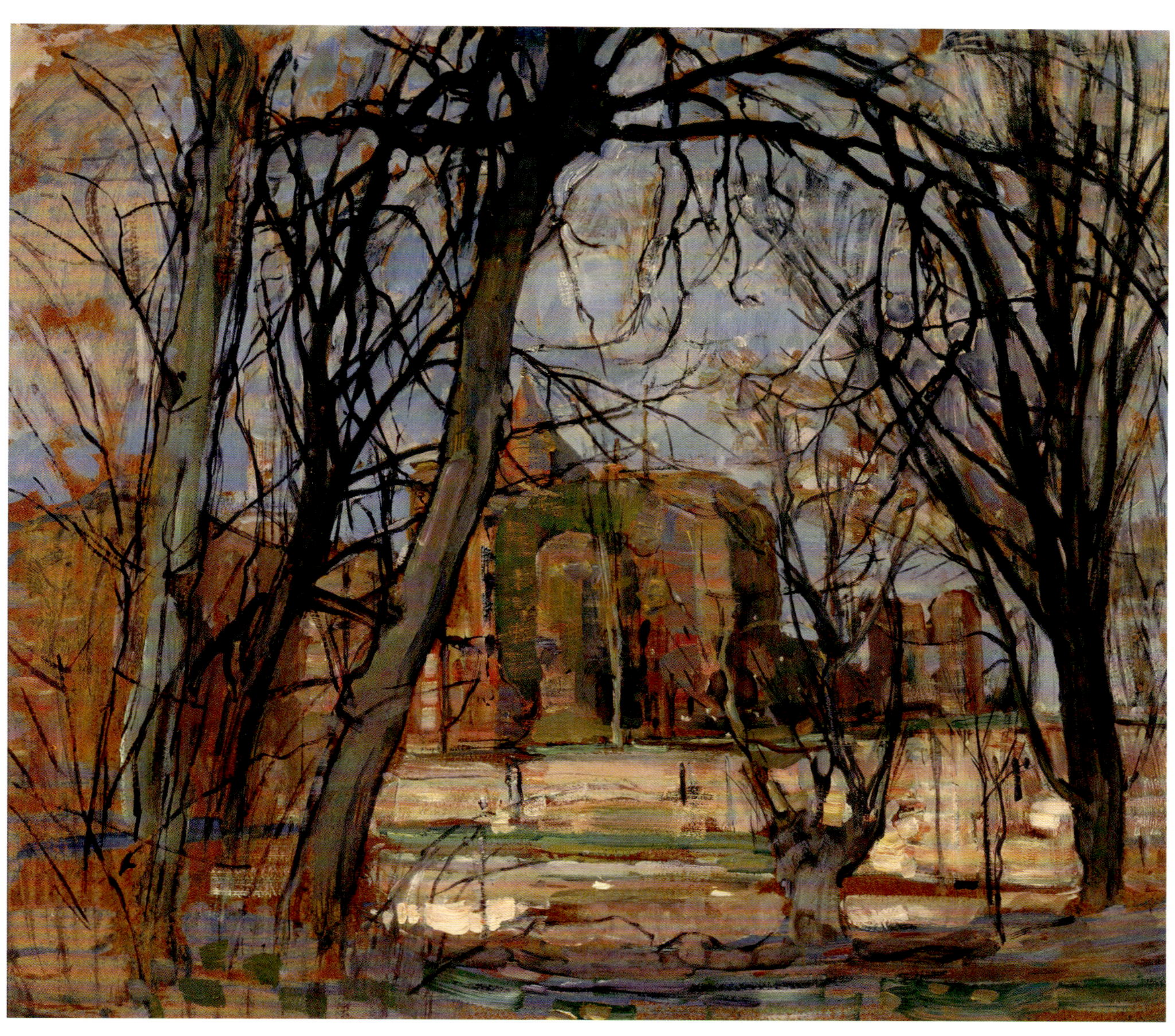

CAT. 39

Piet Mondrian
(born in Amersfoort, Netherlands, 1872–died in New York, New York, 1944)
Spring Sun (Lentezon): Castle Ruin: Brederode
Late 1909–early 1910
Oil on Masonite, 25 × 28 ½ in. (63.5 × 72.4 cm)
Dallas Museum of Art, Foundation for the Arts Collection, gift of the
James H. and Lillian Clark Foundation, 1982.24.FA

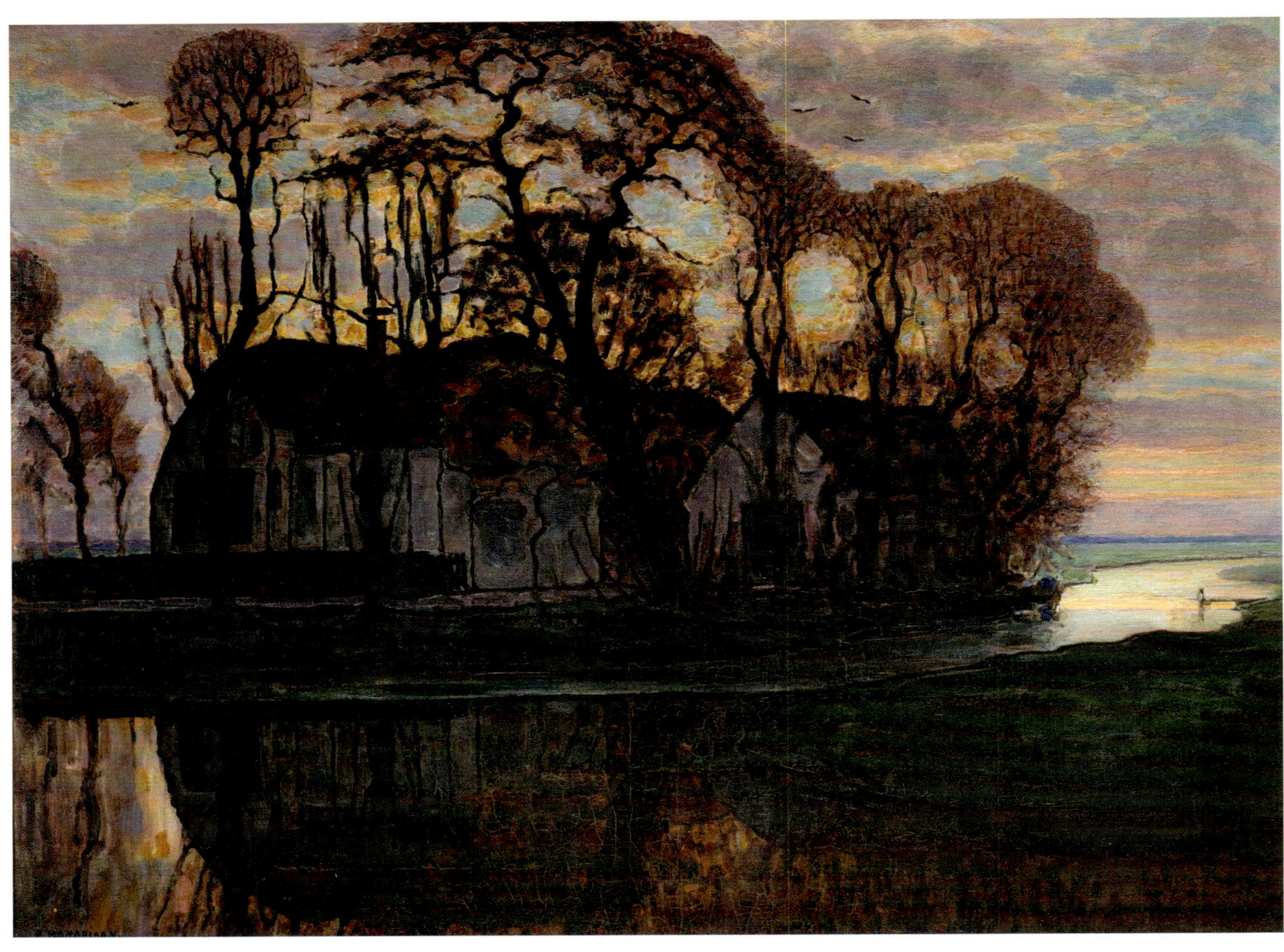

CAT. 40

Piet Mondrian
(born in Amersfoort, Netherlands, 1872–died in New York, New York, 1944)
Farm Near Duivendrecht, in the Evening
c. 1916 (reprise of a compositional series from 1905–1908)
Oil on canvas, 31 ½ × 41 ¾ in. (80.0 × 106.1 cm)
Dallas Museum of Art, gift of the Edward and Betty Marcus Foundation, 1987.359

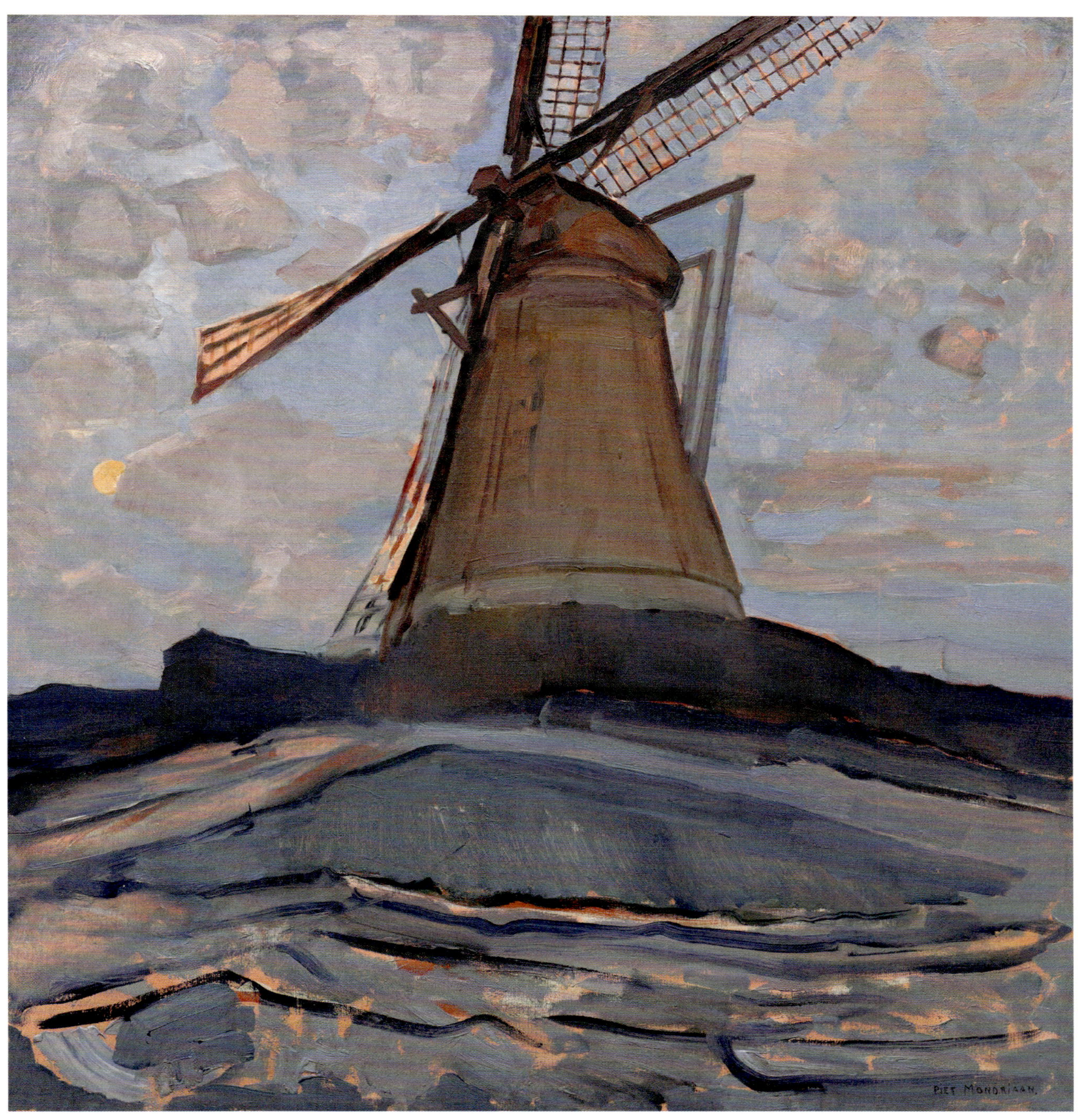

CAT. 41

Piet Mondrian
(born in Amersfoort, Netherlands, 1872–died in New York, New York, 1944)
Windmill
c. 1917
Oil on canvas, 39 ½ × 37 ½ in. (100.3 × 95.3 cm)
Dallas Museum of Art, gift of Mrs. Eugene McDermott to the Dallas Museum
of Art in honor of Mr. and Mrs. James H. Clark, 1989.142

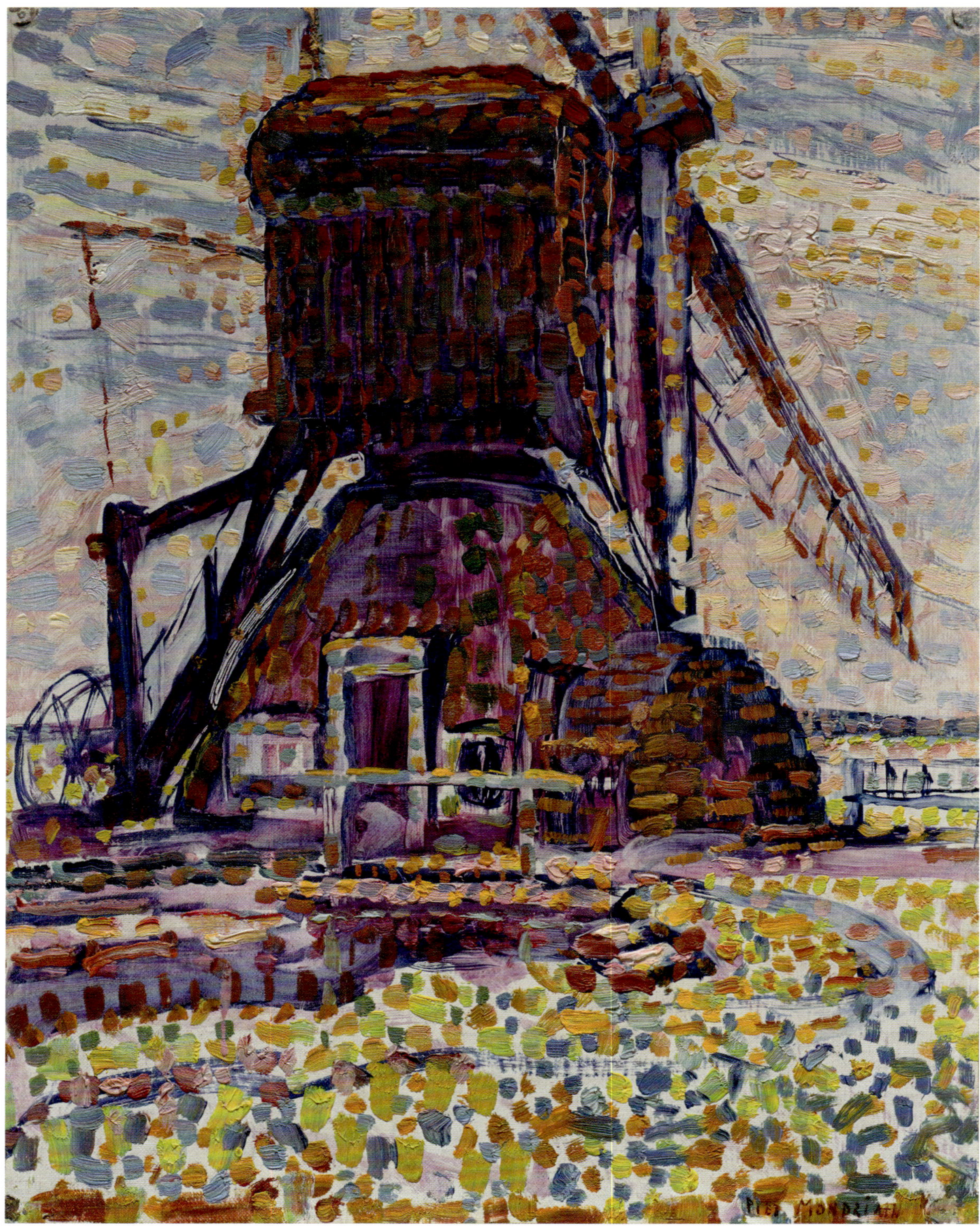

CAT. 42

Piet Mondrian
(born in Amersfoort, Netherlands, 1872–died in New York, New York, 1944)
The Winkel Mill, Pointillist Version
1908
Oil on canvas, 17 × 13 ⅝ in. (43.2 × 34.6 cm)
Dallas Museum of Art, Foundation for the Arts Collection, gift of the
James H. and Lillian Clark Foundation, 1982.25.FA

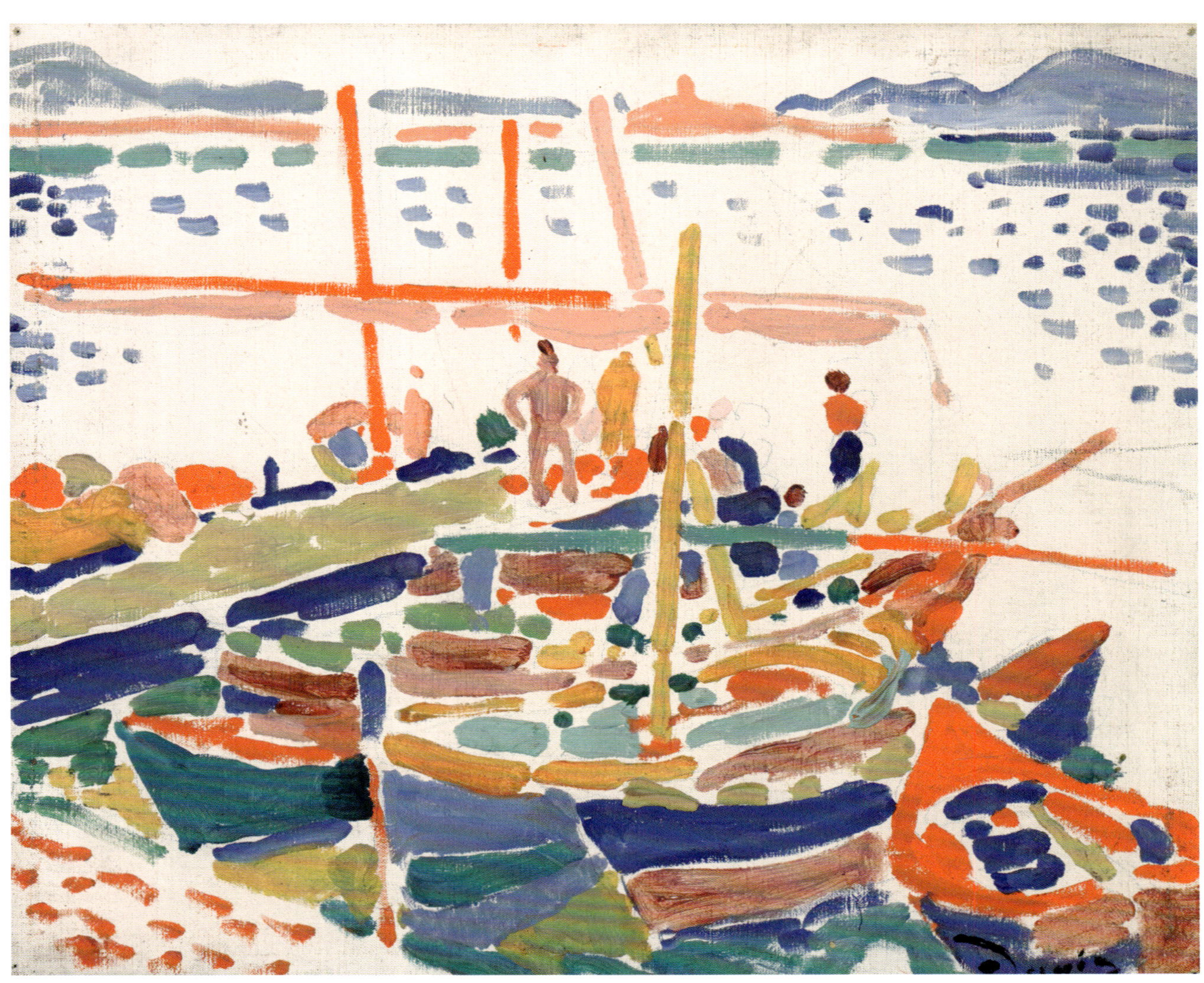

CAT. 43

André Derain
(born in Chatou, France, 1880–died in Garches, France, 1954)
Fishing Boats at L'Estaque
1906
Oil on canvas, 15 × 18 ⅛ in. (38.1 × 46.0 cm)
Dallas Museum of Art, The Eugene and Margaret McDermott Art
Fund, Inc., bequest of Mrs. Eugene McDermott, 2019.67.9.McD

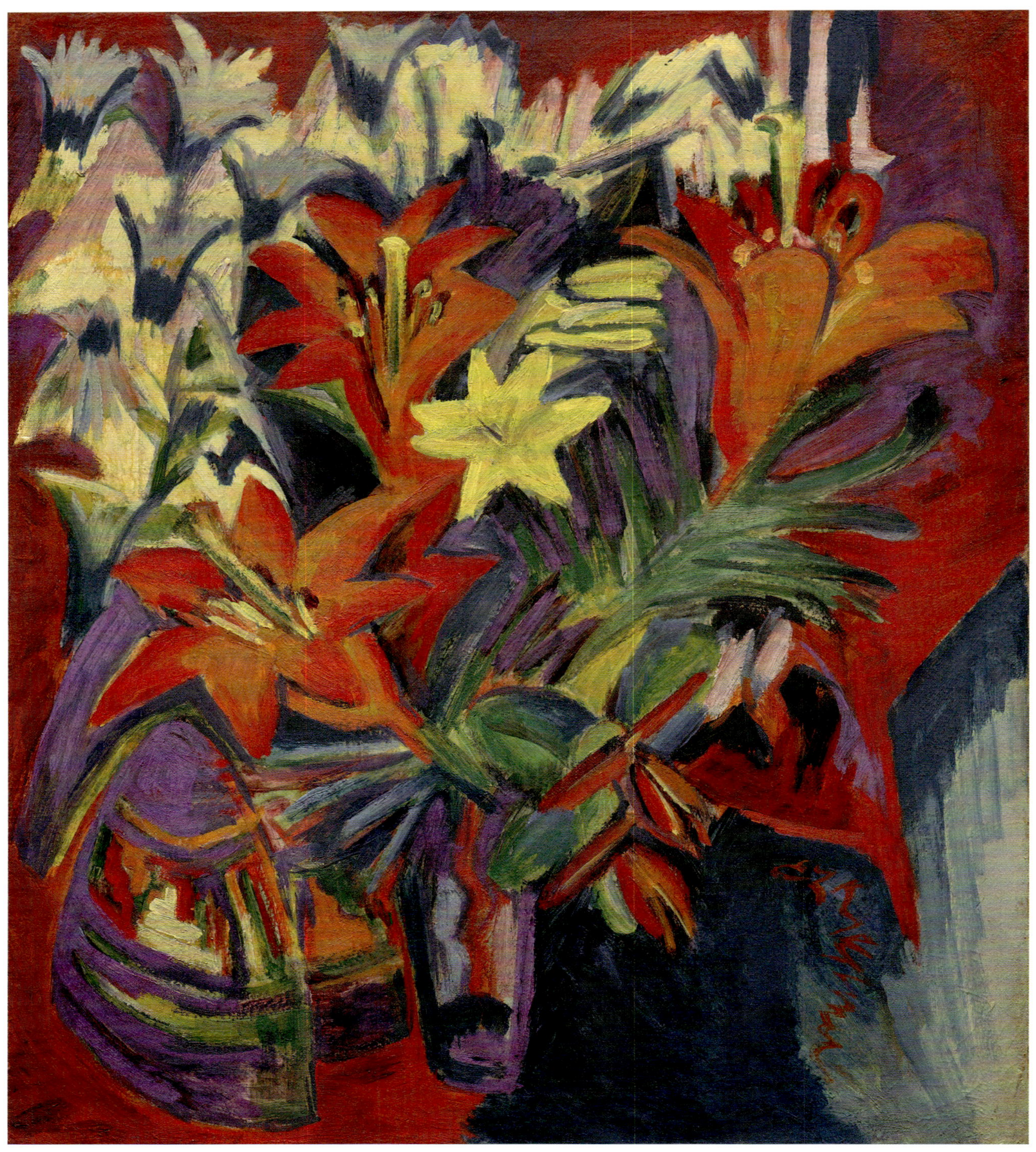

CAT. 44

Ernst Ludwig Kirchner
(born in Aschaffenburg, Germany, 1880–died in Frauenkirch, Germany, 1938)
Still Life with Lilies
1917
Oil on canvas, 31 ½ × 27 ¼ in. (80.0 × 69.1 cm)
Dallas Museum of Art, gift of Cornelia and Ralph Heins in memory
of Elinor Heins, 2019.82.3

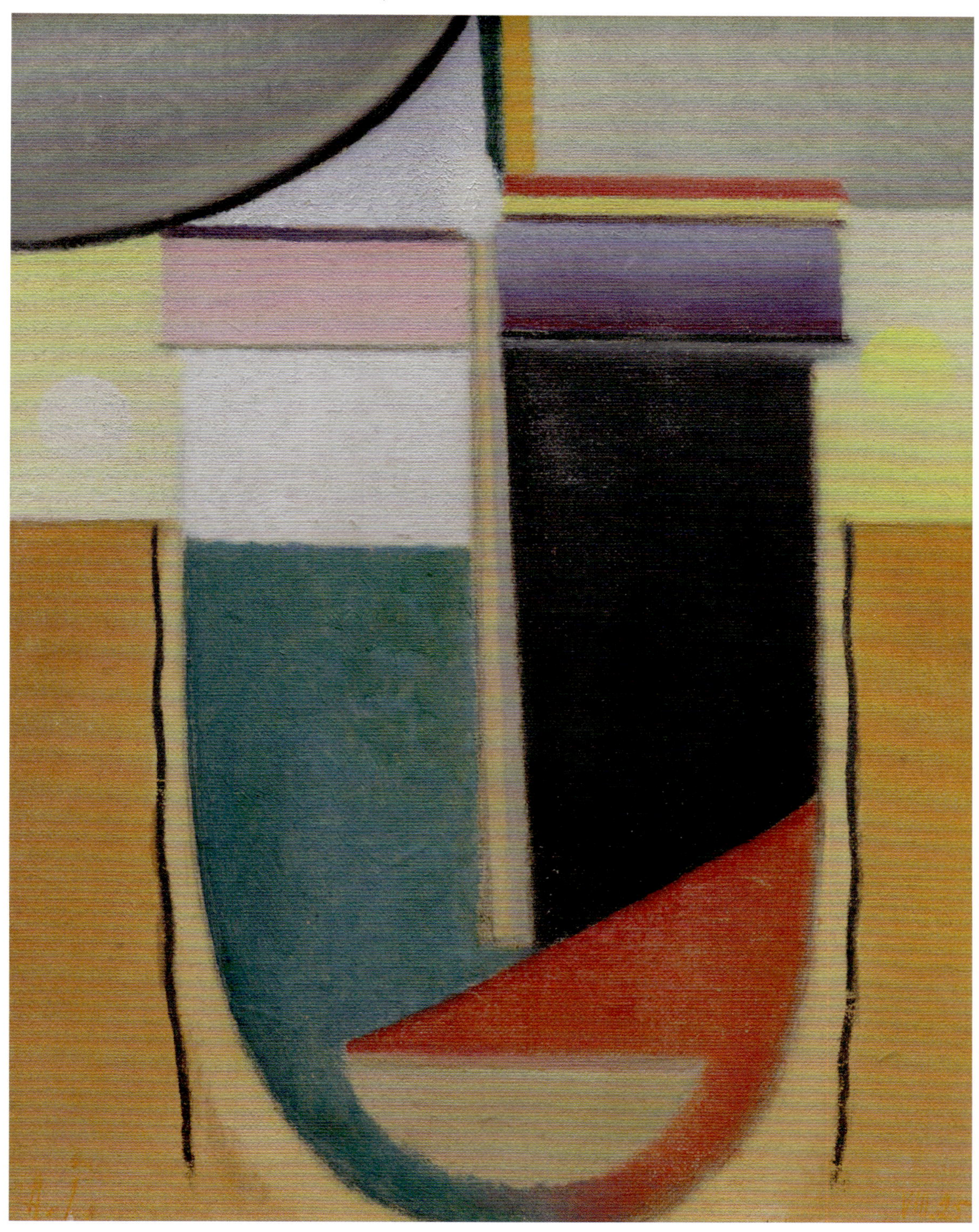

CAT. 45

Alexei Jawlensky
(born in Torzhok, Russia, 1864–died in Wiesbaden, Germany, 1941)
Abstract Head: Two Elements
1925
Oil on cardboard, 17 ⅜ × 13 ⅝ in. (44.1 × 34.6 cm)
Dallas Museum of Art, gift of Cornelia and Ralph Heins in memory
of Elinor Heins, 2019.82.2

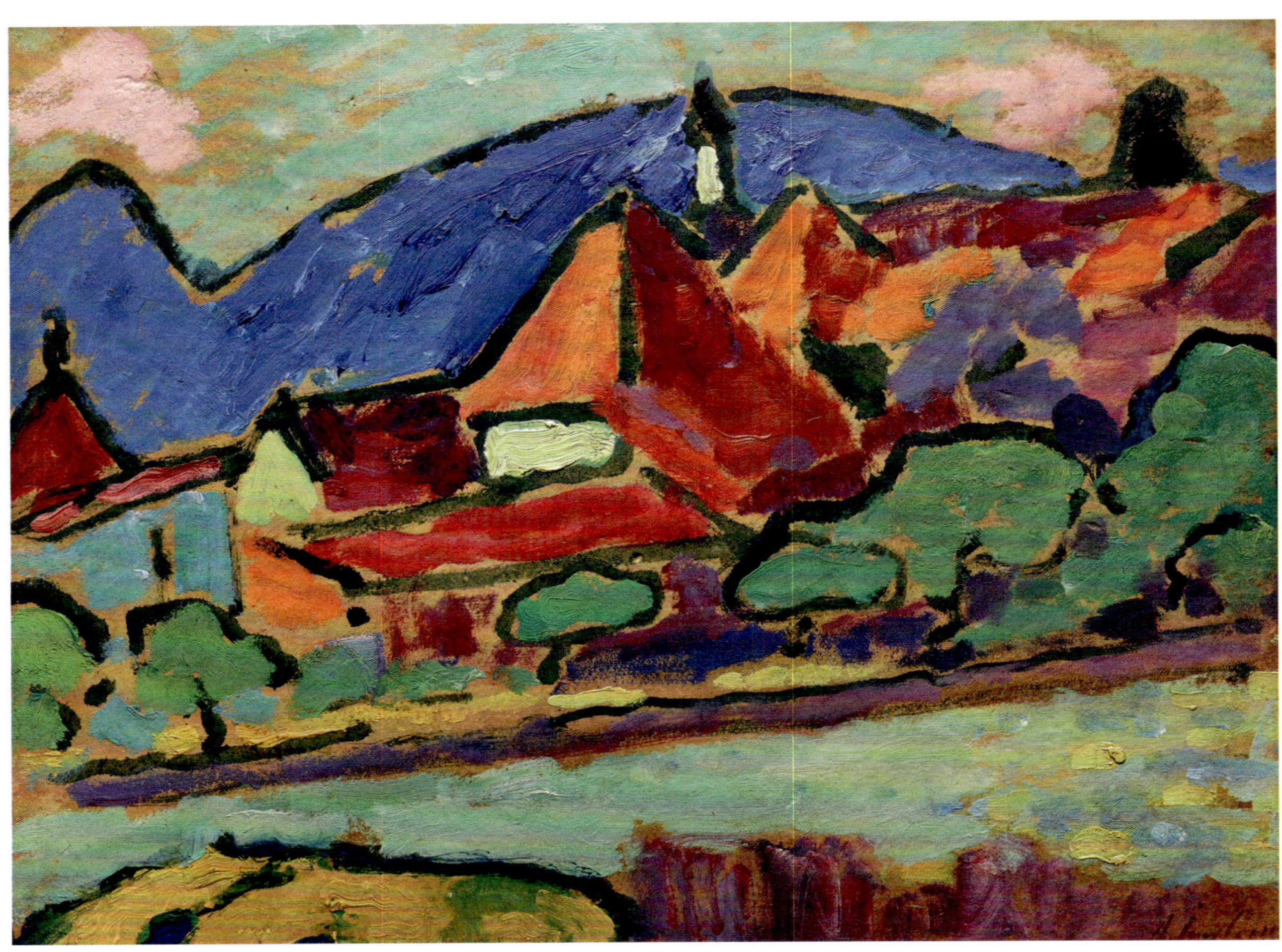

CAT. 46

Alexei Jawlensky
(born in Torzhok, Russia, 1864–died in Wiesbaden, Germany, 1941)

Murnau Landscape
1909
Oil on cardboard, 12 ⅞ × 16 ¾ in. (32.7 × 42.6 cm)
Dallas Museum of Art, gift of Cornelia and Ralph Heins in memory
of Elinor Heins, 2019.82.1

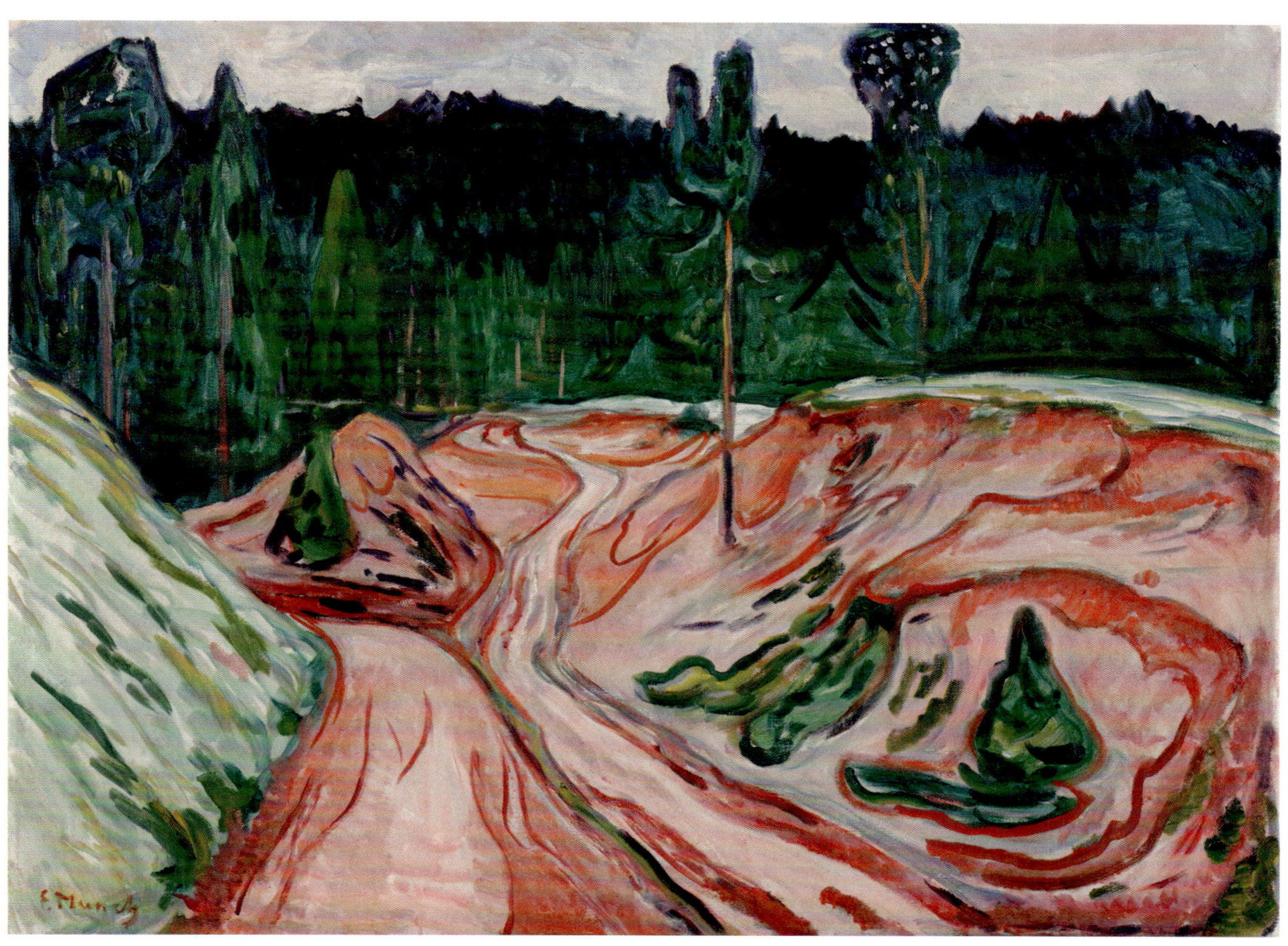

CAT. 47

Edvard Munch
(born in Ådalsbruk, Norway, 1863–died in Oslo, Norway, 1944)

Thuringian Forest
1904 or 1905
Oil on canvas, 29 ¾ × 39 ½ in. (75.6 × 100.3 cm)
Dallas Museum of Art, The Eugene and Margaret McDermott Art
Fund, Inc., bequest of Mrs. Eugene McDermott, 2019.67.15.McD

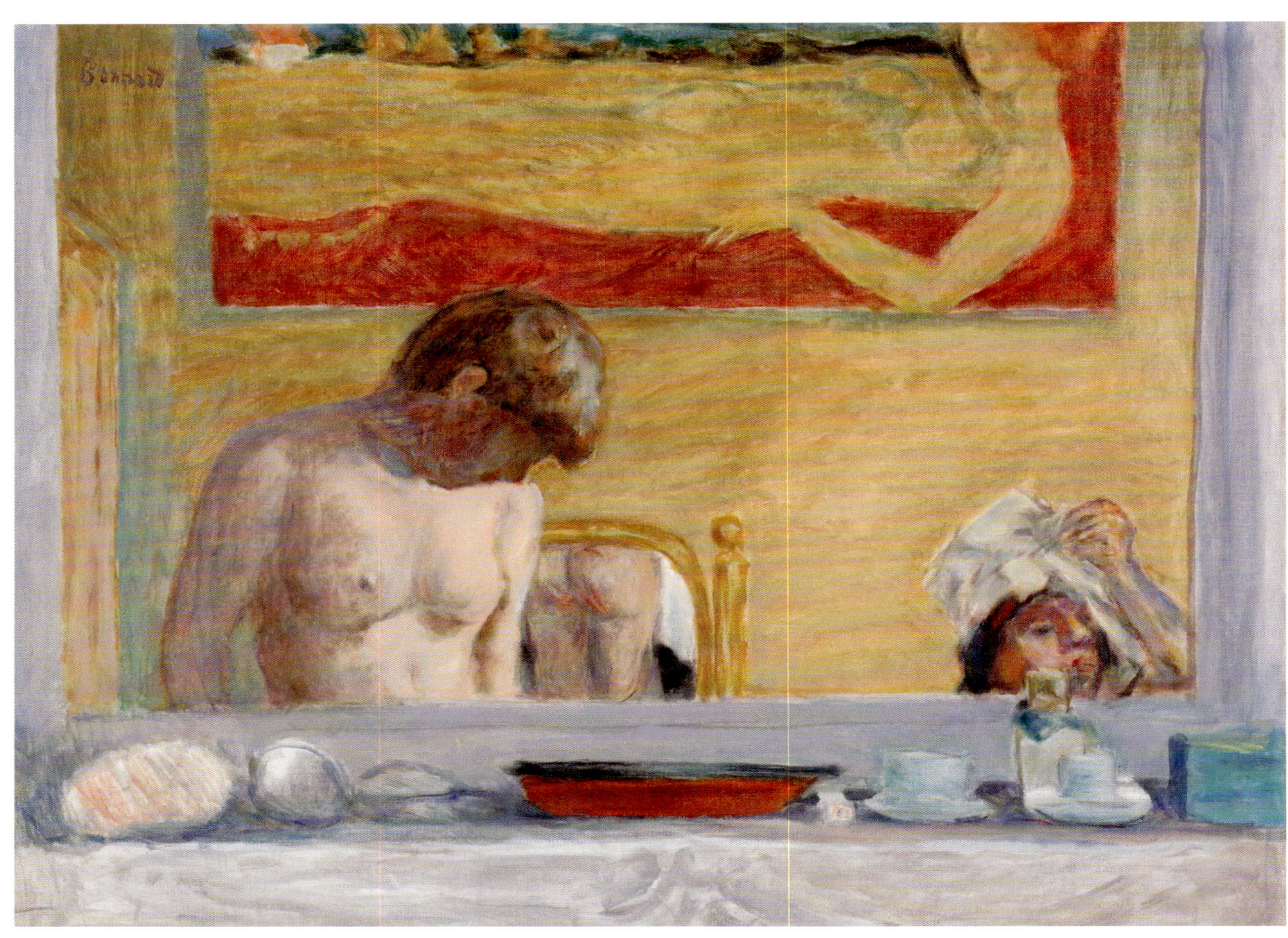

CAT. 48

Pierre Bonnard
(born in Fontenay-aux-Roses, France, 1867–died in Le Cannet, France, 1947)
Young Woman at Her Toilette
1916
Oil on canvas, 24 ¼ × 36 ¼ in. (61.6 × 92.1 cm)
Dallas Museum of Art, The Eugene and Margaret McDermott Art Fund, Inc.,
bequest of Mrs. Eugene McDermott in honor of Marguerite and Robert Hoffman,
2019.67.1.McD

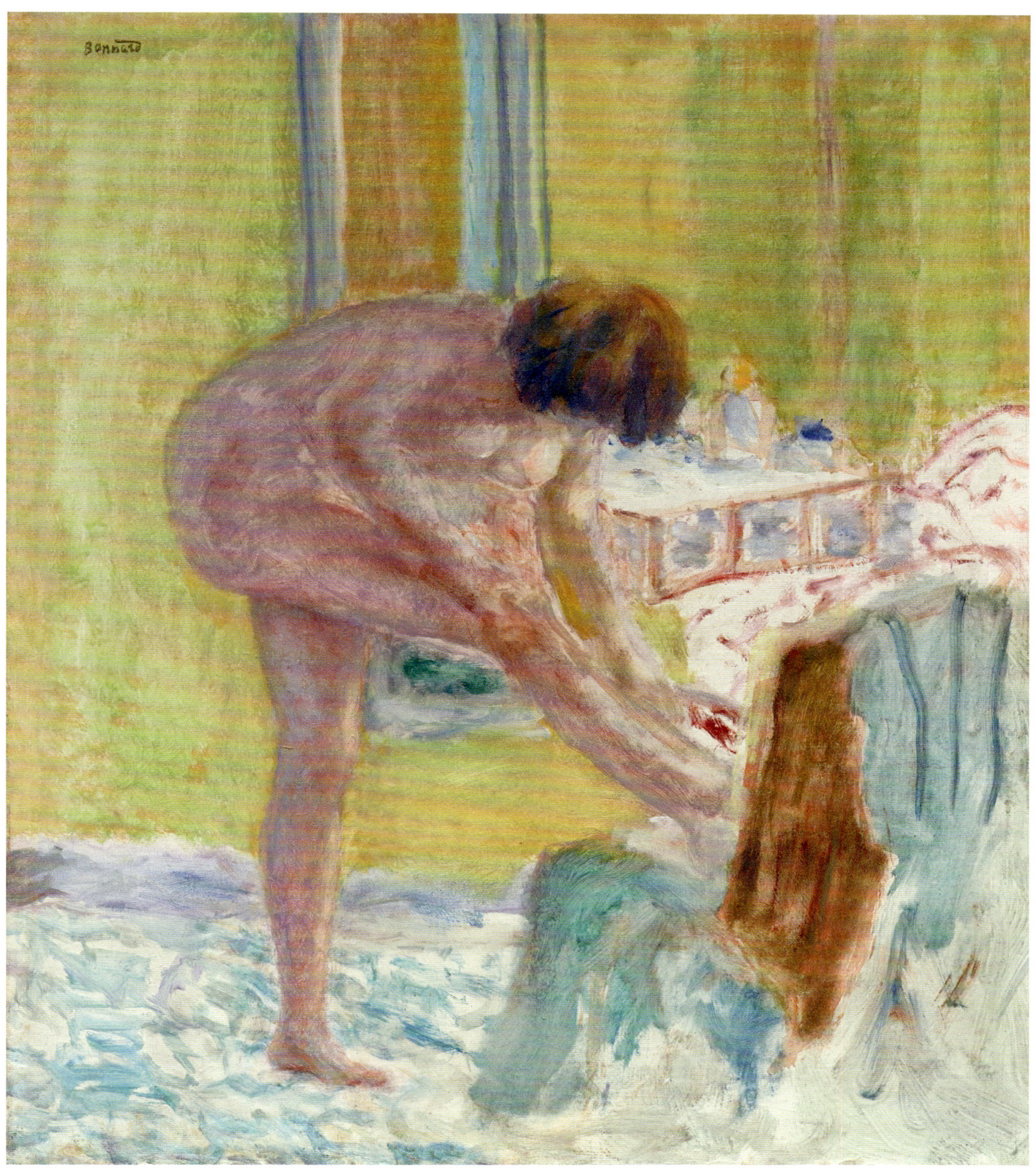

CAT. 49

Pierre Bonnard
(born in Fontenay-aux-Roses, France, 1867–died in Le Cannet, France, 1947)

Nude, Yellow Background
c. 1924
Oil on canvas, 22 ½ × 19 ¼ in. (57.2 × 48.9 cm)
Dallas Museum of Art, gift of the Meadows Foundation, Incorporated, 1981.101

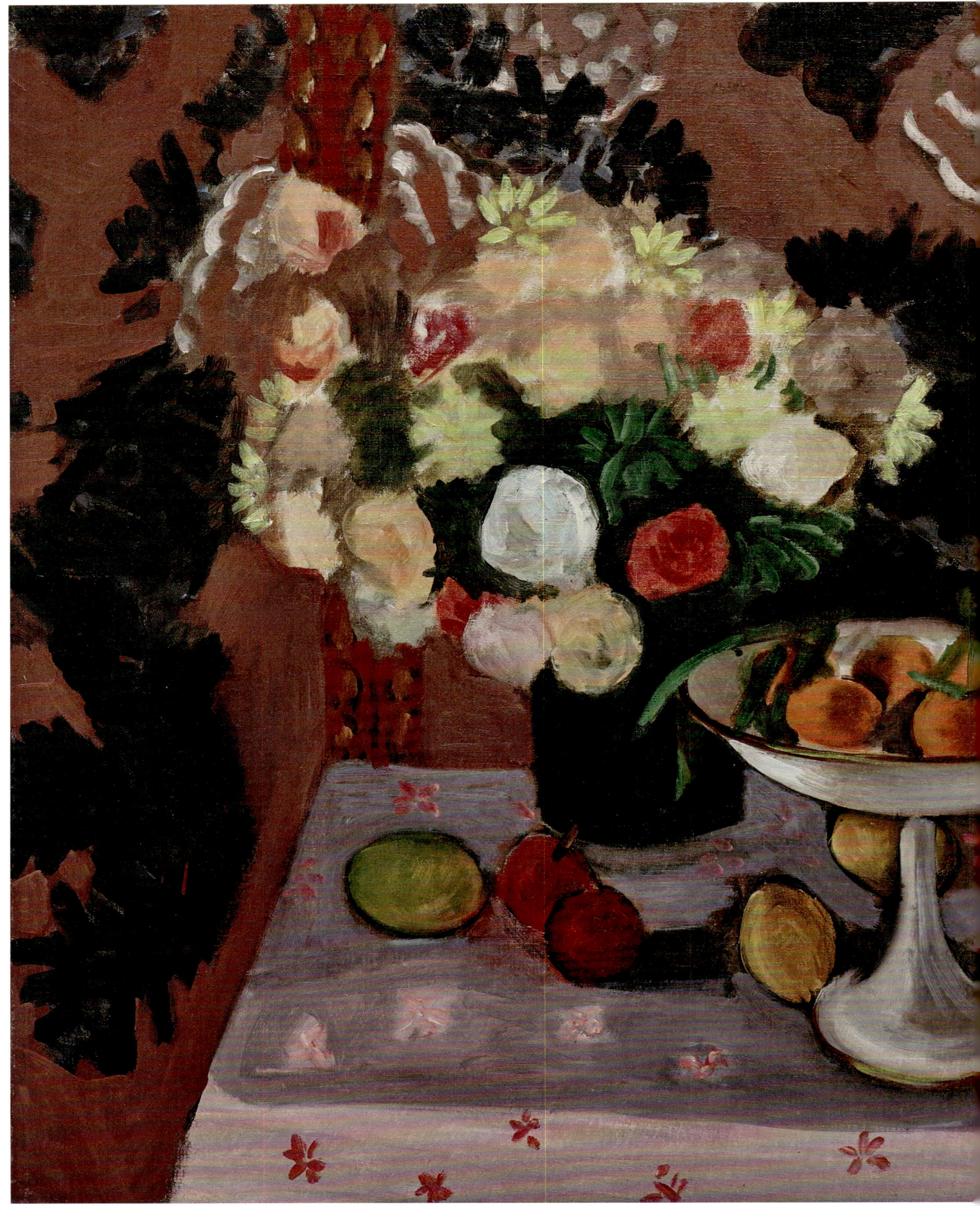

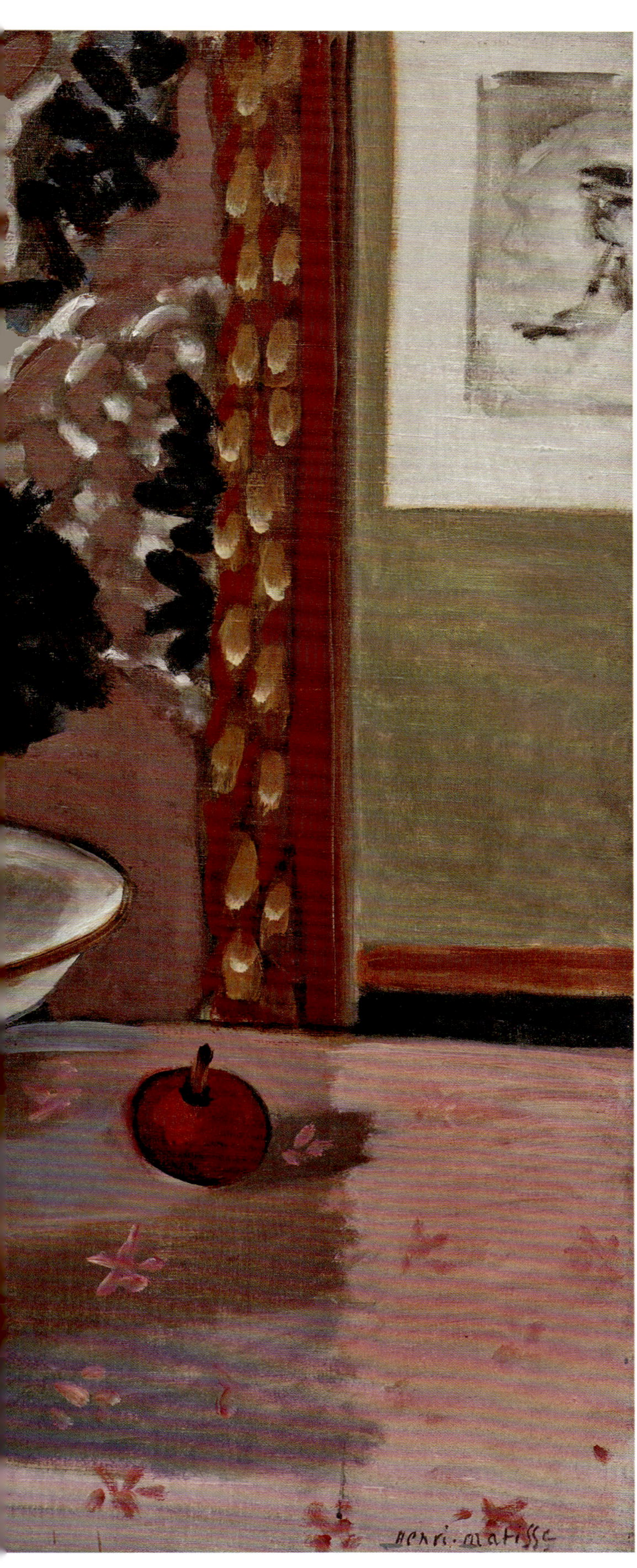

CAT. 50

Henri Matisse
(born in Le Cateau-Cambrésis, France, 1869–died in Nice, France, 1954)
Still Life: Bouquet and Compotier
1924
Oil on canvas, 29 ¼ × 36 ½ in. (74.3 × 92.7 cm)
Dallas Museum of Art, The Eugene and Margaret McDermott Art Fund, Inc.,
in honor of Dr. Bryan Williams, 2002.19.McD

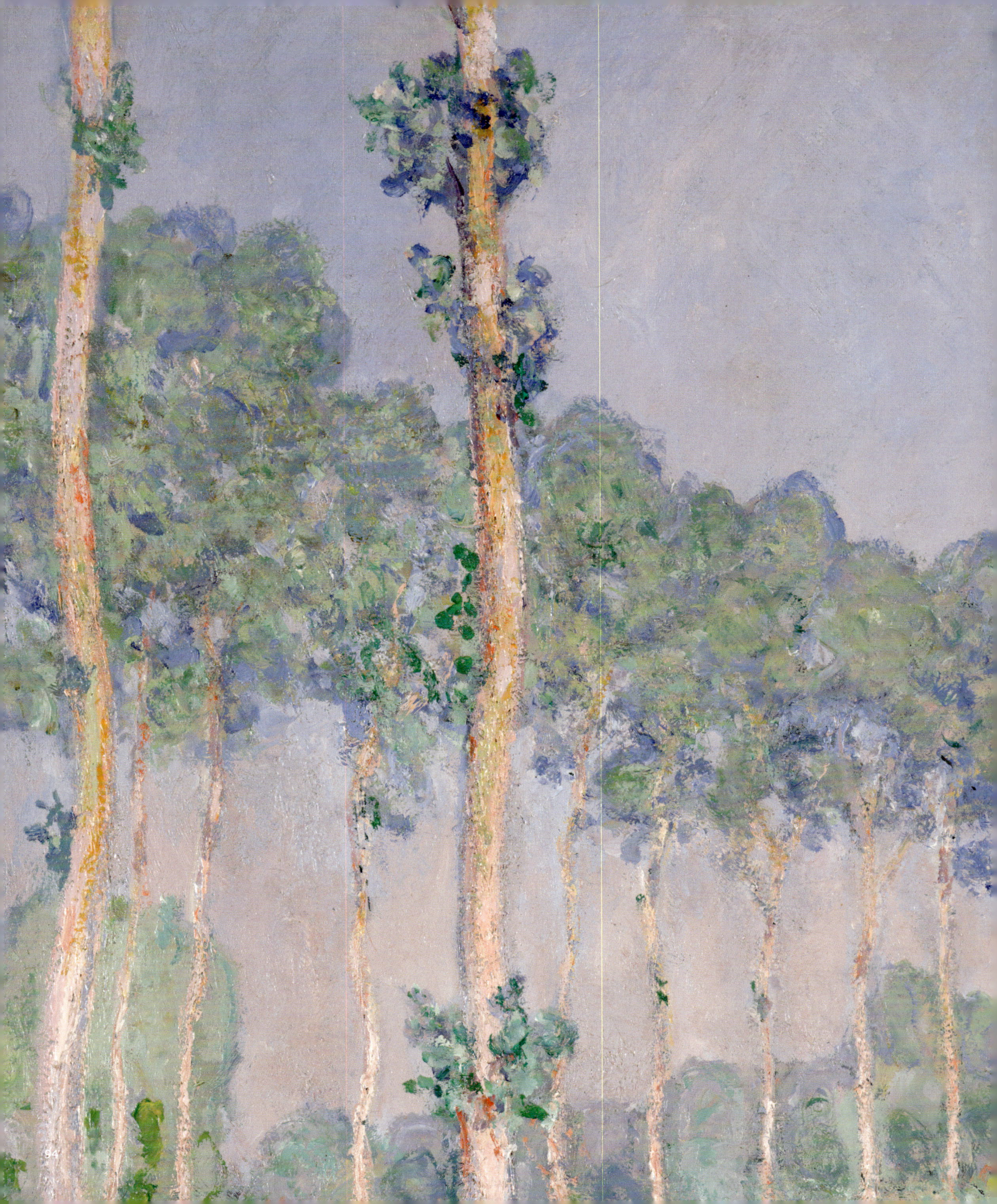

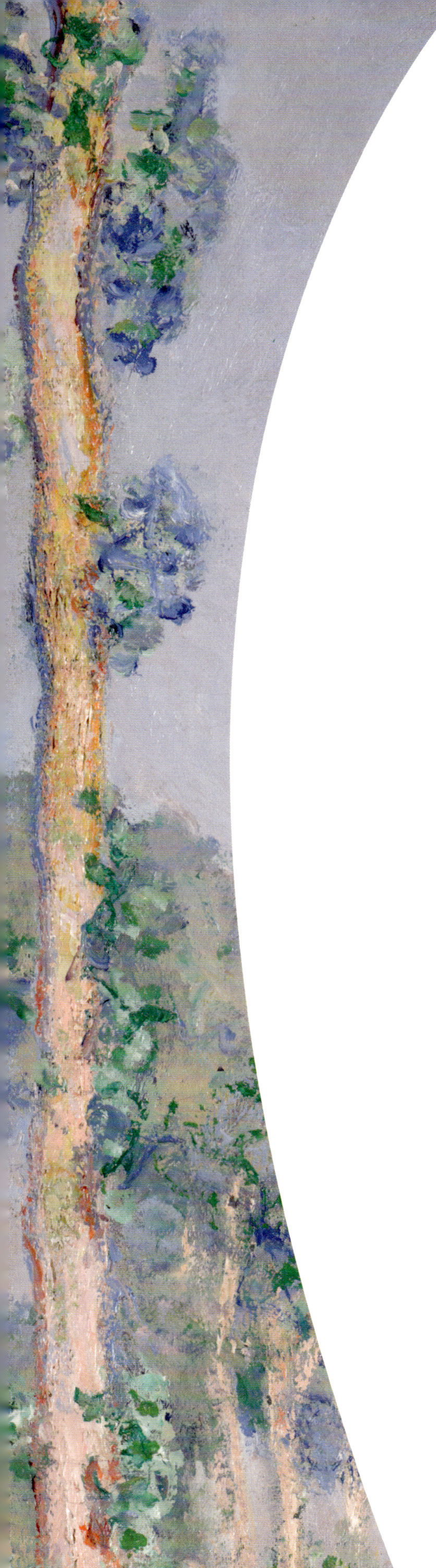

SELECTED BIBLIOGRAPHY

Berson, Ruth, ed. *The New Painting: Impressionism 1874–1886: Documentation*. Vol. 1. *Reviews*. Fine Arts Museums of San Francisco, 1996.

Brettell, Richard R. *Impression: Painting Quickly in France, 1860–1890*. Exh. cat. Yale University Press in association with the Sterling and Francine Clark Art Institute, 2000.

Brettell, Richard R. *Impressionist Paintings, Drawings, and Sculpture from the Wendy and Emery Reves Collection*. Dallas Museum of Art, 1995.

Callen, Anthea. *The Art of Impressionism: Painting Technique and the Making of Modernity*. Yale University Press, 2000.

Howard, Michael, ed. *The Impressionists by Themselves: A Selection of Their Paintings, Drawings, and Sketches with Extracts from Their Writings*. Conran Octopus, 1995.

Kosinski, Dorothy, and Lauren Schell, eds. *Dallas Museum of Art, 100 Years*. Dallas Museum of Art, 2003.

Mainardi, Patricia. *Art and Politics of the Second Empire: The Universal Expositions of 1855 and 1867*. Yale University Press, 1987.

Mainardi, Patricia. *The End of the Salon: Art and the State in the Early Third Republic*. Cambridge University Press, 1993.

Myers, Nicole R., ed. *An Enduring Legacy: The McDermott Collection of Impressionist and Modern Art*. Dallas Museum of Art, 2018.

Patry, Sylvie, ed. *Inventing Impressionism: Paul Durand-Ruel and the Modern Art Market*. Exh. cat. National Gallery Company, 2015.

Patry, Sylvie, and Anne Robbins, eds. *Paris 1874: The Impressionist Moment*. Exh. cat. Musée d'Orsay and National Gallery of Art, 2024.

Pitman, Bonnie, ed. *Dallas Museum of Art: A Guide to the Collection*. Dallas Museum of Art, 2012.

Shields, Caroline, ed. *Impressionism in the Age of Industry*. Exh. cat. Art Gallery of Ontario; DelMonico Books-Prestel, 2019.

Stevens, MaryAnne, ed. *After Impressionism: Inventing Modern Art*. Exh. cat. National Gallery Global, 2023.

Tinterow, Gary, and Henri Loyrette. *Origins of Impressionism*. Exh. cat. Metropolitan Museum of Art, 1994.

Venable, Charles, ed. *Dallas Museum of Art: A Guide to the Collection*. Dallas Museum of Art, 1997.

Weitzenhoffer, Frances. *The Havemeyers: Impressionism Comes to America*. H. N. Abrams, 1986.

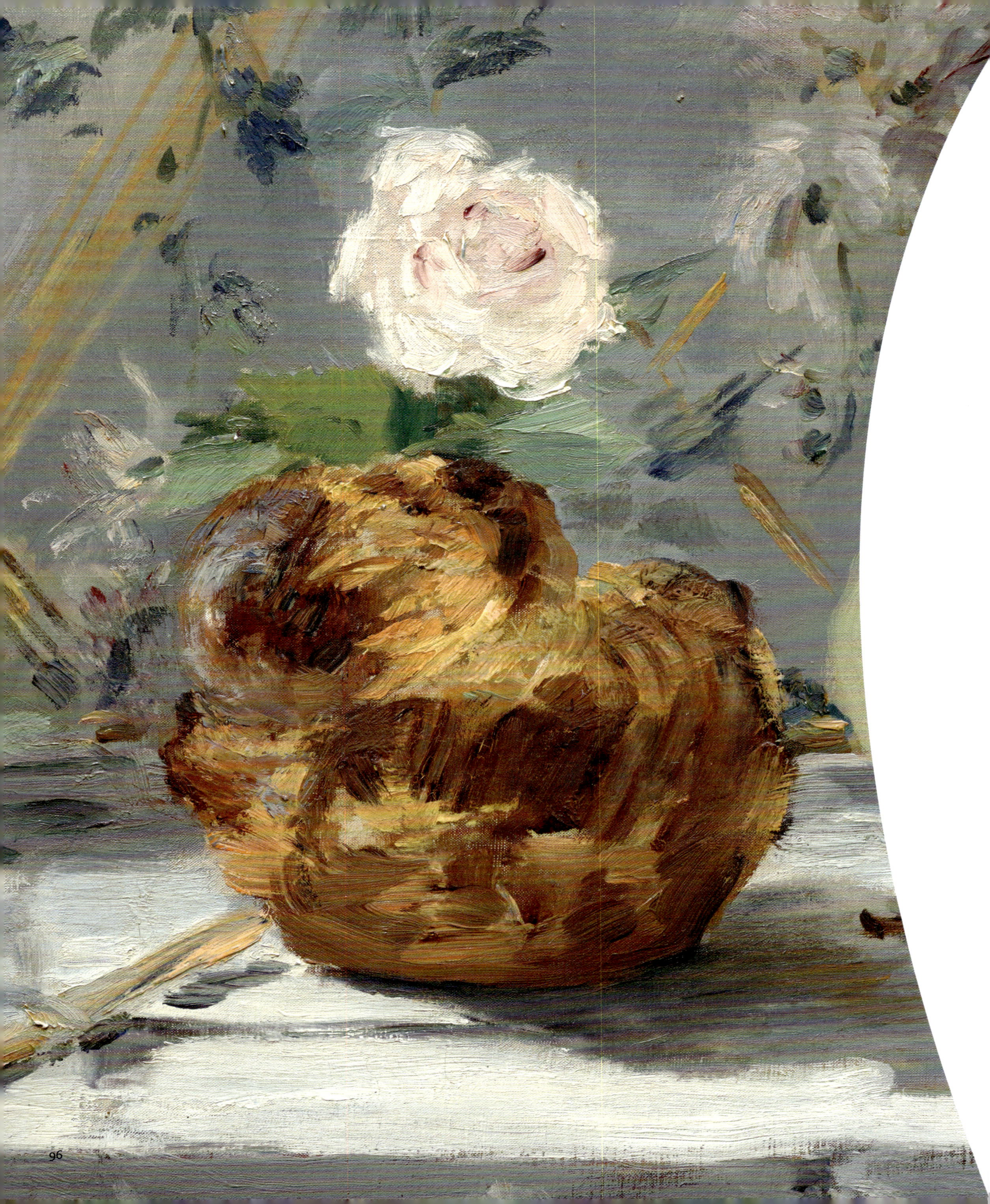

NOTES

That 1870s Show

1 Cham, "Impressionist Exhibition," *Le Charivari*, 1874. Author's translation.

2 Louis Leroy, "L'Exposition des impressionistes," *Le Charivari*, April 25, 1874, cited in Berson 1:26. Author's translation.

3 Bertall, "Exposition des impressionistes," *Paris-Journal*, April 9, 1877, 1–2, cited in Berson 1:131. Author's translation.

4 Albert Wolff, "Le Calendrier parisien," *Le Figaro*, April 3, 1876, 1, cited in Berson 1:110. Author's translation.

5 Bertall, "Exposition des impressionistes," cited in Berson 1:131. Author's translation.

6 Argus, "Chronique," *La Semaine des familles*, April 21, 1877, 47, cited in Berson 1:123. Author's translation.

Monet to Matisse at the Dallas Museum of Art

1 For a more detailed discussion, see "That 1870s Show" on pages 10–17 of this volume.

2 Paul-Armand Silvestre, "Le Monde des arts: Exposition de la rue des Pyramides (premier article)," *La Vie moderne*, April 24, 1880, 262, cited in Berson 1:306. Author's translation.

ILLUSTRATION AND COPYRIGHT CREDITS

Details

Front cover, top right: Claude Monet, *The Water Lily Pond (Clouds)*, 1903, see cat. 19, p. 52; middle left: Claude Monet, *The Seine at Lavacourt*, 1880, see cat. 16, p. 48–49; bottom right: Camille Pissarro, *Place du Théâtre Français: Fog Effect*, 1897, see cat. 2, p. 31

Frontispiece: Claude Monet, *The Water Lily Pond (Clouds)*, 1903, see cat. 19, p. 52

Pages 6–7: Paul Signac, *Comblat-le-Château, the Meadow (Le Pré), Opus 161*, 1887, see cat. 25, p. 60

Pages 10–11: Gustave Caillebotte, *The Path in the Garden*, 1886, see cat. 12, p. 41

Pages 18–19: Claude Monet, *Water Lilies*, 1908, see cat. 20, p. 53

Pages 28–29: Camille Pissarro, *Place du Théâtre Français: Fog Effect*, 1897, see cat. 2, p. 31

Pages 44–45: Berthe Morisot, *The Port of Nice*, 1891, see cat. 22, p. 55

Pages 58–59: Paul Signac, *Mont Saint-Michel, Setting Sun*, 1897, see cat. 27, p. 62–63

Pages 64–65: Louis Anquetin, *Woman at Her Toilette*, 1889, see cat. 30, p. 68

Pages 78–79: Henri Matisse, *Still Life: Bouquet and Compotier*, 1924, see cat. 50, p. 93

Pages 94–95: Claude Monet, *Poplars, Pink Effect*, 1891, see cat. 18, p. 51

Page 96: Edouard Manet, *Brioche with Pears*, 1876, see cat. 4, p. 33

Back cover, top left: Eugène-Louis Boudin, *Open Sea*, 1889, see cat. 15, p. 47; middle right: Claude Monet, *The Seine at Lavacourt*, 1880, see cat. 16, p. 48–49; bottom left: Alfred Sisley, *Street in Ville-d'Avray*, 1873, see cat. 23, p. 56

Published in conjunction with the exhibition titled *The Impressionist Revolution: Monet to Matisse from the Dallas Museum of Art*, organized by the Dallas Museum of Art.

A variation of this exhibition titled *The Impressionist Revolution from Monet to Matisse* was presented in Dallas February 11–November 3, 2024, and was co-presented by Texas Instruments and PNC Bank. The Dallas Museum of Art is supported, in part, by the generosity of DMA Members and donors, the Texas Commission on the Arts, and the citizens of Dallas through the City of Dallas Office of Arts and Culture.

CO-PRESENTED BY

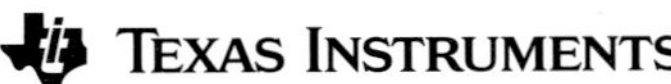 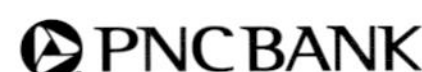

MAJOR SUPPORT

Freeman Family Exhibition Fund

CONTRIBUTING SUPPORT

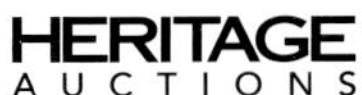 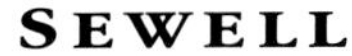 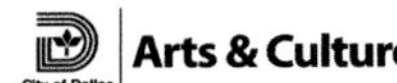

EXHIBITION SCHEDULE

Dallas Museum of Art
February 11–November 3, 2024

Museo del Palacio de Bellas Artes
March 24–July 27, 2025

Santa Barbara Museum of Art
October 5, 2025–January 25, 2026

Frist Art Museum
February 27–May 31, 2026

Virginia Museum of Fine Arts
November 14, 2026–March 14, 2027

Queensland Art Gallery | Gallery of Modern Art
June 19–October 4, 2027

Dallas Museum of Art

Tamara Wootton Forsyth
Interim Director/The Marcus-Rose Family Deputy Director

Nicole R. Myers
Chief Curatorial and Research Officer and
The Barbara Thomas Lemmon Senior Curator of European Art

Amanda Dietz Brooks
Head of Exhibitions and Publications

Veronica Treviño Salinas
Exhibitions and Publications Project Manager

Edited by Queta Moore Watson

Designed by Boldface Studio, Plano, TX

Typeset in Adorn Condensed Sans and Prenton PR Pro
by Boldface Studio

Color management by Friesens

Produced by Boldface Studio

Printed and bound in Canada by Friesens

Published by the Dallas Museum of Art
www.dma.org

Distributed by Yale University Press, New Haven
and London
www.yalebooks.com/art

© 2025 Dallas Museum of Art

Library of Congress Control Number: 2024943098

Authorized Representative in the EU Details: Easy Access System Europe, Mustamäe tee 50, 10621 Tallinn, Estonia, gpsr.requests@easproject.com

ISBN 978-0-300-28003-6